MAVERTONS MAVERICS

Nigel Hansen

A.K.A   SMURF

THE AUTHOR.

A 60 year old ex International truck driver, living in Colchester, England. Retired and disabled due to Emphysema.

Nigel has been married for nearly 40 years, and still wonders how his wife Joan has stayed and put up with his travels and some of the scrapes and brushes with the law throughout Europe and the Middle East, during his 35 years on the road. And working for some of East London's gangsters.

2 sons and 6 grandchildren now settled down to home life, and his fish pond. Has decided to put his life and times on paper. This is his second book, and gives a day by day account of one of many trips to Iraq and back, overland. His first book. Burning rubber, a trucker's life. Is a quick look into his life and the jobs that he has had.

This book he has made more factual, drawing from notes and diaries that he has kept over the years. He has not softened or taken anything out, this is all the good and bad times, and the stunts that were pulled to get the job done. Legal and not so legal.

This is dedicated to.

My wife Joan. Who has put up with me for so long, and stood by me all the way.

My two sons Darren and Mark. Who I missed most of their early years growing up through being away in some country or other.

All six of my grand children. The only word of advice to you all is stay the hell away from trucks kids.

Just another trip

Its 3am as I get out of a nice warm bed and get dressed. Try and creep down stairs so as not to wake the boys up, that's not easy to do in this house as every bloody floor board creaks. Joan comes down as well and makes a coffee as I have a quick wash and shave in the kitchen sink. Then we go through the same routine every time I leave on a trip. Have you got this that and the other, is everything in the car and lastly, have you got your money and passport.

The hardest part of the whole trip is from the front door till I am in the car and driving off. I have to get this over quick or I will not go. A kiss, yes I love you, yes I will phone you from the yard. (I never do) And I will phone you from Rotterdam tonight. Another kiss and then a dash to the car and I am on my way. Next stop the yard at North Farm, Loughton. It's more like winter than spring, as it chucks it down with rain all the way. The yard as I pull in and park up looks like a ploughed up field. And there's my truck parked in what looks like a lake. That's all I need at the start of a trip. I get the truck as close to the car as I can, then start putting everything into the truck, and trailer boxes. Just finished and walking over to the office, and I end up on my ass in the mud, fuck it. Back to the truck, a pair of overalls and back to the office. Kettle on while I sort out my paperwork, and get it in some sort of order. That finally done I change out of my jeans and pants and into the overalls. A quick coffee and back to the truck. It feels as if Joan has starched these overalls. I will have to get out of these at Felixstowe.

Not a bad run across to Romford and up the A12 and A45 to Felixstowe, all the traffics going the other way. A bit of luck there's a customs officer at the truck park on the terminal, and I get him to seal the trailer and belly tank, only he don't want to get under the trailer and get wet, so he gets me to do it for him. Reminding me to make sure that the tap is turned off when I seal it. Of course I will officer. Customs office everything stamped up, then over to book myself onto the ferry. Only time for a coffee out of the machine, as they want me on board now. I am the last on, good that means that I will be first off and be able to park near the Dutch customs office for the night.

After checking in with the purser and getting my cabin, I stick my jeans and pants in the ships laundry. A good shower and a couple of pints with the lads up in the bar before dinner. Then duty frees, and a bit more. The extra being Marlborough about 600. Enough to get me to the first Coricom in Bulgaria. Then it's time for a quick nap before getting in at Europort and our evening meal, before getting off the ferry. Everyone makes their way down to the truck decks, and as I pass the pursers office I collect my jeans and pant. All clean, dry and ironed. Then it's off onto Dutch soil and over to the customs office. All the paperwork done I change my mind there are too many Dutch truckers about and all on the beer, so I have decided to give it the big one and get down to the other side of Frankfurt then park up and sort out my tacho cards, and really give it the big one from there on through. I want to see just how much I can shave this run down. And without the aid of popping stay awakes.

Two cups of filter coffee and I am on my way out of the dock and down past Kantars bar onto the highway to the Rotterdam Ring. As soon as I am on the motorway its pedal to the metal all the way. Centre lane to Dordrecht, through the tunnel and on to Breda. Switching lanes and motorways to Tilburg and Eindhoven.

Not dropping below 90 Km P.H. I switch again now for the last bit in Holland to Geleen and into the Shell truck stop at Heerlen. The Dutch German border at Aachen Nord is only 500 yards away, and the Germans watch this place, so it's a good hour break and as they have seen me pull in and then pull out an hour later, they will not want to see my tacho cards. Thinking that I am all legal. I am at the moment apart from the speed. I do tend to try and keep legal in Germany as much as possible, as it gets expensive. While I am here I phone Joan, its midnight back in England and she will still be up waiting for me to call to let her know that I am OK. Then she will go to bed. But she will expect a call every time that I can till I get into the Eastern Block.

15 minutes in the customs and that's both Dutch and German done and I am on my way again. I had spent my time making out the tank shine for the fuel on the truck and the Lau settle for the Germans, and they just stamped them not even bothering to check them. I could have fiddled loads of fuel if I had known that would happen, Gits. That was now 4 ½ hours driving done and I was on my way to Frankfurt. Only two motorways so I get my foot down. Ease off as I come past the motorway police station at the Aral services before Koln and drop down

the hill. Over the Rhine and down to the split for Frankfurt. This motorway is one hill after another. And there is one that I am looking out for. The cats back, just before Limburg. There is a 40 Km P.H. limit for trucks on it, and it's under camera all the way down and up, and no overtaking. I forgot all about it once, and got the fright of my life. It had been a pitch black night, 2am and I was in the centre lane when half way down the heavens light up like daylight, and this voice from nowhere says, "English if you hear me put your left hand out the window." I do it, and then it says "good we see you at the service station, if you make it". I got waved into the services and there was the helicopter just landing.150 D Mark that cost me, a lot of money in 1973. There was no way that hill was going to catch me out again.

It's getting light and traffic is starting to build up as I near Frankfurt so I ease up on the speed. Pass the airport and pull in the services, find a gap between a couple of trucks and park. Time for a coffee then a couple of hour's kip before going on. I want to make Geiselwind truck stop today, so I take the tacho card out ready to put a new one in that has already got 10 hours sleep on it from a tacho under the bunk. This tacho is only wired up so it will only record sleep and both are set at the same time. So it's nearly impossible to tell the difference.

3 hours later I am awake and have changed my mind by the time I have had a quick wash and cup of coffee. I am going to start cutting some time off this trip. I am going for the border at Rozvadov into Czechoslovakia. Not stopping at Geiselwind or Nurnburg. But punch it through to Schwandorf and take an hour's break there, before going to the border and with a bit of luck I should catch them at shift change.

That's 4 hours stuck on this poxy motorway at Nurnburg without moving. When these krauts have a motorway pile up they have a good one. They go out and kill a few people. There's 15 cars in this one, mind what can you expect from a load of nutters all doing over 100 M.P.H. This means there could be a problem at the border. The German customs will know about this and may start asking for tacho cards. It's a change of plan again. Safer to park up at Schwandorf Autohoff for the night and go through early hours of the morning, as they will be half asleep still.

There it is the iron curtain. Half a mile in front of me as I sit here at the German customs having a coffee waiting for my papers to be done. A 12 foot high wire mesh fence topped with razor wire, and armed watch towers every 500 yards, that's without the electric fence and mine field. And these Czechs' and Russians have levelled this half mile gap of everything, to give their border guards a clear killing field. And once you crossed through that fence, you went back in time. This was the last place that I could phone home to Joan, for at least four or five days. At least till I got to the National Hotel in Belgrade.

I pulled forward and up the road to the gate into the East. Showed the Russian officer my passport and drove through to the truck park, outside the customs office, got my papers and walked in. There he was. Shit for brains, then he saw me and called over, "he English you got big problem this time". I just looked at him and then pointed at him. And with my other hand I drew it across my throat in a cutting motion. He took the message, and walked away. "The Czech is not your friend mister." A tall Russian officer comes over, shakes my hand and takes my papers. 15 minutes later all my papers are done, as is my visa, and we are sitting down having a cup of coffee. Like all Russian military officers on the borders they all speak near perfect English. I used to joke with them, saying that it was always good to have a friend in the K.G.B. When you had to deal with idiots like these. If the officer had a red stripe down the side of his trousers he was KGB. And he was the one to see if the local idiots gave you grief.

Coffee over we shake hands and I am on my way. I will try for the border at Bratislava tonight and stop there. But that plan got changed 3 miles further on up the road. Shit for brains is standing by his Skoda waving a little stop sign at me. No chance, as I aim the truck at him, and watch as he dives out of the way. He is game. He is after me in his car now. Now he is not only stupid but dangerous. He comes up the inside of the trailer and is stabbing at the tyre. There is a bang as the tyre blows, and bits of Skoda go flying out into the field. That's 110 Lb per square inch pressure that has hit him blowing the trailer tyre and him into oblivion. A mile up the road and I pull in and round the back of a small truck stop. Two packets of Marlborough and I get my tyre changed, while I get myself a coffee. These are not the best of roads but I am not about to hang around. Through Pilzen and away round the Prague ring road, past a police man who thinks better than trying to stand in front of a speeding truck and stop it, and waves me past telling me to slow down. Well I think that's what he was saying.

Midday and I pull in the other side of Brno for a break. I am only just putting the kettle on as another Brit pulls into the rest area along side me. He hasn't stopped since leaving the border. Apparently a customs officer is in hospital badly injured after coming of the road in his car. But he had a message for me from a Russian officer, not to come back that way again. Well let's hope that nothing has got to the border at Bratislava about it. Coffee and a bacon sandwich and it's time to get rolling again, no more stops till the border.

There are four trucks in front as I pull in and join the queue, with the city of Bratislava over to the left of us and that iron curtain with its watch towers on our right, and Austria. Ahead was Hungary and Rajka border post. Through the Czech no problems here, 500 yards to the Hungarian weigh bridge. Now I have to pull a stroke to get past this. I am a bit over weight on the drive axel so what I have to do is get the Brit that is following me to slowly pump the cab over very slowly while I am still inside and drive the truck slowly over the axel weigh bridge, and when the drive axel is clear drop the cab back down. With the cab tilted forward it lifts the weight off the drive axel by putting it forward, so I am not over weight entering Hungary on the drive axel. This costs me three packets of Marlborough and a new pair of Joan's tights, and the young Hungarian girl border guard get a kiss as she gives me the weighbridge ticket. Now I am in a fairly civilised part of Eastern Europe and we are through and on our way to Gyor. The other Brit wants to stop for the night at the Plane, but me I am going to the Hotel Wien on the outskirts of Budapest. The plane has to many girls on the game and it is not safe there overnight. At least at the Wien you can phone home and get a good shower cheap, and the police are around at night. So we part company and I go on.

Great there it is, as I swing hard right off of the main road and down the service road to the hotel. Hard right at the end, and back up along the side of the hotel. I am totally knackered, that's the whole of Czech in a day. Tomorrow could be cancelled, but I know that I will be in Belgrade at least two days. So I will go when I wake up, that means no alarm calls. Can't be asked to make a coffee so grab my wash gear and change of clothes, and head over to the hotel for a shower and coffee. This is the first change of clothes since getting off the ferry at Europort, and my first shave. By the time I get back to the bar for a coffee I feel like a human again, and I must smell a bit better as the girls behind the bar even talk to me.

The sun is shining as I wake up, and all the trucks have gone. Over to the hotel and a quick wash to wake up and a couple of cups of coffee, and I set off again. Only as far as Kecskemet, where I pull in at the Shell garage to fill up the truck and the belly tank with black market fuel. I have bought coupons for 200 Lt plus I want about another 600 and I am hoping that I can get at least 3 to 1 and the coupons. That way I get 800 Lt for 200 D Mark. Just done the deal and two pumps on the go as a police car pulls in, drives round and then drives out the same way he pulled in. That was a close one. Full and a free coffee, I am on my way again. Not bothering with stopping at the windmill, as this place is ruined now as the Turks and Rumos have started using it. We the Brits have found one down near Szeged. The old girl there soon chases the others out, and it's only a couple of miles from the border with Yugo.

Both sides of the border are empty, not even a car. I don't even see anyone walking about, this is a bit strange. When I walk into the customs office they are all there, and half cut. It's a national holiday but if I want to go it will cost me a pack of Marlborough. Five minutes and I am through. The Yugo side is just the same, only these want two packs. Papers done I have a coffee at the bar before going on. But have a couple of hour's kip first. Three hours later I am awake and on my way. This country is expensive as far as communist countries go and very corrupt. They would sell their own mothers if you paid them. Our fiddle with them was the transit tax. That was 50 -50 as was the motorway toll. A coffee stop at Novi Sad, then the run into Belgrade. Off the highway at the first exit after the airport, bear right and right at the roundabout down the long narrow drive to the National Hotel. Here it was get yourself turned round and parked up best you can. And never leave your truck windows or doors open or unlocked even if you were chatting down the side of it to another driver. It was midday when I pulled in and parked up. That feat had taken 20 minutes and 8 shunts to jack knife round and park.

The National Hotel Belgrade. Anyone ever called this a nice place is a liar. This place is the pits. The only people that came here were thieves prostitutes' and truckers, and we only came here to get visas, faxes and phone calls. Mind you they were monitored by the police. You could hear them in the back ground. Or you could get mail here, like one letter that was sent here for me but picked up by a mate and taken back to Joan. Did I get it when I got home? On the way back from a trip I had called in at the National and ended up giving two young English girls a lift back to Dover. They were good they paid for all the meals and coffee all the way back. Well they sent a letter to me c/o the National hotel. Only thing was they not only thanked me for the lift but enclosed a couple of photos of themselves in bikinis and how they wished I had tried it on as they were willing. I got ear ache for the week that I was home, and my mate nearly became an ex mate. Did he ever grovel and apologise.

Early on the second day I started up and pulled out. Apart from phoning Joan and the yard there was nothing I needed to do there, so I left and headed for Nis where I stopped for a break before going on to the Bulgarian border at Dimitrovgrad. But I wanted to be through this bandit ridden country in one go border to border. The only hold up would be round Sofia and Plovdiv. And how right I was. Into the country was a pain in the neck. Customs wanted the side of the trailer open. Why? In case anyone wanted to come to Bulgaria illegally. Of course I upset them, when I told them that no one wanted to come in. The Bulgarian people wanted to get out. That was clever of me. 2 hours later I got my papers back. Next hold up was on the Sofia ring road. Giving it the big one, foot flat to the floor there's the police, and this prat standing in the middle of the road with his hand up. He wants me to stop. Everything, all my brakes lock on and there's smoke coming from my tyres, there's that much smoke I can't see behind me and this prat is still there. He moves at the last minute and I manage to pull in 100 yards past him. And walk back to him. All the time I am swearing and calling him all the names going. And grab hold of him by his collar threatening to kill him next time. All he is saying is speeding, radar. Over and over pointing at a cardboard box in front of his car. He nearly started crying when I stamped his radar flat. It wasn't till he started waving both his arms around telling me to go, that I noticed he was holding his pistol. I let him go, patted him on the shoulder and walked back to the truck and drove off. What the fuck was I doing? That little Lada had no chance of catching me; I should have just kept going. I never saw one cop all the way to Svelingrad or when I parked up at the Coricom between the town and the border for the night. I would let the night rush go through, and then I would drive into the border when it was quiet.

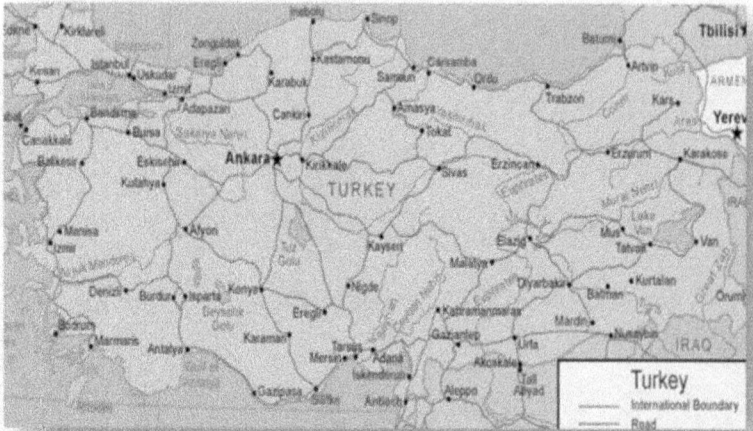

GATEWAY TO THE MIDDLE EAST.

Once through the Bulgarian customs you enter the world of the Turk. This is like stepping into another world. At least the people back on the other side of that iron curtain had some semblance of common decency and morals and manners. Here it all got left behind and forgotten. Here it is survival of the fittest. Up you Jack I'm ok.

Kapikula. What a customs post this is. To get through this maze of ever changing autocracy. As it is never the same, it depends as to the individual customs officer, and what his brain power is, and how short of cash and cigs he is. The sight of Western currency, Dollars especially will work wonders, as will a couple of packets of Marlborough.

The first thing you do on parking up amongst the other couple of hundred trucks is find Young Turks Runner. Young Turk is the customs clearance agent that we Brits use. Normally this young lad of his will have seen you come into the compound. You give him everything; passport as well as he will get your visa done along with your papers. Here your truck details go onto your passport, you can't get out without your truck. What you don't do is try and do the customs yourself. I did it once, and it took me two and a half days 100 Dollars and ten packets of cigs.

The customs building is a corridor running round the outside of a square, in this square sit 12 customs officers, each desk is numbered and you have to go to each of these desks. Only there is a sequence, and the only people that know it are the customs, and it changes with each shift. So let young Turks lad do it. You will be away within 6 hours. So after numerous cups of Turkish chi (tea) in small glasses that you burn your fingers on holding it, and walking round the street market, buying junk that you didn't need in the first place. The young runner finds you and hands you your papers back and your passport. Now all you have to do is get your truck over to the exit gate, get your trailer seal checked, T.I.R, paper stamped and signed and your away. First stop is the Londra camp, just up the road on the left, and pay Young Turk and give the lad a packet of cigs. By now it's too late in the day to get to Istanbul in day light, so you go and park up with the other trucks.

Londra camp Kapikula. A long single story building with transport offices, shops, restaurant, bar and a bank. And right in the middle is the Londra camp hotel, with its telephones and telex. And most important is the showers for the drivers that are at the back of the building. And if you use them, your braver than me. What you do is about four of you book a room in the hotel for the night and use the one in the room. Then you also have the use of the roof top pool, as do all the other drivers. At the back of the truck park there is a truck wash and workshop that you can get the truck serviced and tyres repaired or changed, but me I will do all that at the Londra camp in Istanbul. It's time now for a shower, meal and a few beers. Efes the only beer that I know that never seems to have the same alcohol content in each bottle.

Early morning and it's time to go. A quick splash of cold water to freshen up and a couple of cups of coffee to get the caffeine back into the system, and then we are away. Into Edirne and turn right for Silivri and Istanbul. Now what you have to do and the local cops are waiting for you to do it. Is put your foot down and get done for speeding. Pay the fine, a couple of ponds in Turk Lire, and go like mad for the rest of the day, only don't forget to stop at the T.I.R, check points and get the control paper signed and stamped, for if you miss one. You will get sent back to get it done. I pull in at the Silivri check point and park at the back and have a brew. This check point is at the junction with the road from Ipsala on the Greek border, and is overlooked by an old castle on top of the hills. From here it's an easy drive into the Londra camp if you start driving like the locals. Every one of them is certifiable as a homicidal maniac. As long as they have that sign up in their windscreen. Masalah they will be ok. Down the hill past the airport and into the next check point just before the Mobil camp, where all the Bulgi and Rumo drivers stop. A short drive up to the start of the city and there is the Londra camp. A big white four story block. Turn right and stop at the entrance to the truck park. I hand the security my international driving licence, get the date and time ticket and drive in and park down on the right hand side, with all the other Brits and Scandinavians and Dutch. This place is like Kapikula but on a bigger scale. All I want is a drink and a meal. Tomorrow I will cancel and wash and service the truck and trailer. And check the brakes as there are a few nasty big hills to go over.

Over in the bar restaurant there are a few Brits sitting down having a beer, while they wait for the restaurant to open so to be sociable I join them in a beer. I notice a young lad sitting on his own on the far side of the restaurant, so I call him over to come and join us. Turns out that it's the lad's first trip. Not just to the Middle East, but out of England. And to top it all, it's his first driving job. He was driving for Falcon Gate from Liverpool. A good outfit, but he had come with two others. Sub contractors, and they had been winding the lad up all the way down about the bandits and getting shot up by them. That's when Charlie Prior walked in and said "the only bandits out here are those two, Andy on Cantrell's and the smurf on Mavertons." As he sat down and put another six beers on the table. I took the beer, and then asked prior when I was likely to get my spare carnet back. By the end of the night the lad was sorted. He would go with one of the Davies Turner drivers in the morning.

It must have been about four or five in the morning when we were all woken up by a load of girls screaming and laughing. Top Deck Travel had just pulled in with a load of Australians. The Aussi drivers were told where to go in two words. And the second one was off. Old London transport double Decker bus kitted out. Sleep upstairs eat and live down stairs. Aussi drivers based in London, and running overland to Australia and back, their passengers all students and they were a bloody nuisance. They knew that they were not allowed in the truck park, or use any of the trucker's facilities. As we regularly hauled them out starker's from the showers. They could use the hotel not ours. And the drivers often had the water turned off at the truck wash; they could use a bucket and brush. To say that they were not well liked would be an understatement, and they were not impressed when we called them our colonial peasants. Or ex cons that really pissed them off.

That day I spent checking every bulb, all the tyres and brakes then had the cab up and changed the fuel and oil filters, and checked the fuel water trap and even went as far as checking the diff and gear box, and greased the trailer and unit fifth wheel. Stuck my dirty washing in the laundry and showered before having a meal and a beer.

Everything's done and 1870 miles from home, another call to Joan is in order. As there is only two more places that I can get a call back to the U.K and its another six days to Zakho and a good eight days to Baghdad. I am only just over half way, on the outward part of the trip.

Its 5am and I am pulling out of the Londra and down the hill to the Bosporus Bridge. This bridge is identical to the old River Seven Bridge at Chepstow, right down to the toll booths. It's only when you have crossed to the Eastern side that you are in the Middle East, and have crossed from Europe to Asia. Up the hill to the first check point. Now to give it some down the hill and past the Ford truck factory, as that's where they will be waiting. There he is side of the road waving me in, and he has got the ticket ready. There's one more check point before going up Bolu, so I stop and have a break there. That's when the cop tells me that there was a bad accident in the night. And that the road is still closed for another hour. They have to clear all the traffic first.

Christ why send a young lad out here on his first trip out of the U.K. There it is at the bottom of a 200 foot drop. Falcon Gate. Just hope he didn't suffer. The two D.T drivers are at the top by the check point with the police. As I go to the check point one of the lads calls out that he will see me at the Telex later, I put my hand up to him and carry on down the other side. And even after seeing that the kamikaze are still at it, passing on blind bends and going flat out down this mountain who's road is no more than a dirt track, with the odd bit of tarmac here and there. And the most dangerous of them is the inter city coach drivers. As far as they are concerned they are the only people on the road. A quick stop and brew up at the bottom by the checkpoint then on again. One more check point before the Telex Motel Ankara and an overnight stop. Two hours later the two D.T lads pull in. By the time they park up and come up to the bar I have two large Brandy's waiting for them.

They see it happen. Tonker in his over loaded truck was overtaking on a bend when he clipped one of the D.T trucks, and went straight into the side of Falcon Gates cab pushing him off the side of the mountain, and going over himself. So in a way there was justice. But now they had to get hold of Falcon Gate and tell them, so that they could inform the lad's family. And get things organised to get the lads coffin back. That would all be done by Falcon Gate. And a collection box was set up on the bar by Yusuf the owner of the Telex for the lad's family. A first timer but one of us. There's at least one Brit trucker killed every month out here doing this job. But you can't let it get to you. You have to keep going. This is the bit they miss out in the truck driver's manual. This death and all the others out here will not make the Sun newspaper. The only time they support truckers is when they can make money out of truckers, they never put their hand in their wallet.

Early the next morning there's a slow departure of trucks from the Telex, and I am about the last to leave, and head south to cross the salt flats before the sun starts to really heat up. In and out of the check point and on we go. Two hours later I drop down through Death Valley and out onto the salt flats. There are still a lot of

Flamingos left out there, so there must still be some water that's not been evaporated in this bloody heat. I pull over and park by the old ruins and try to get the truck out of the sun while I make a brew. I am joined by one of Astrans drivers, Clive. An ex barrister. There are a lot of strange drivers on Astrans. People that you would never think of as being truckers. There's doctors, dentists, lawyers, airline pilots, teachers. You name it there here working for Astrans as drivers. OK they are the best Middle East road transport company going, and have the finest backup system out here for their drivers. Saying that, one of their drivers had a heart attack and died in his truck in Munchen. Didn't find him for three days. Then it was the German police that noticed the truck hadn't moved. But there is one thing that Astrans are famous for and that is the TV film that they did for the BBC or ITV. They had three of their trucks on a trip from their base in Kent to Riyadh Saudi Arabia. No problem. They went their normal route Greece, Cyprus, Syria, Jordan, and into Saudi at Al Amari, across to Turayf and then followed the pipe line H4. There is no soft sand anywhere along this road. It's just rock and scrub, but the film crew found soft sand. They drove off the tarmac road and down into a dry river bed just so they could show them digging themselves out, to make the film interesting. Even Astrans bosses try not to mention it. But to us they are film stars, idiots but film stars.

Clive and I part and go on our way. Him to the Telex at Ankara, and me to the checkpoint at the foot of the Taurus mountains the other side of Aksaray, in the village of Ulukisla, as it will take all day to get over these mountains and down into Adana. This mountain has taken a lot of unwary truckers. The road is steep, narrow, twisty and bad. This is one mountain that you really respect.

After a good night's sleep and a wash with the cold water from the village well and a glass of chi with the old men sitting outside the tea shop, it's time to go. As dangerous as this road is the kamikaze are still at their old stunts. But this is one mountain that I will not back down from them and give way. I hold my line and stay there, I will not move over. At the top I pull in at the check point and put the kettle on for a brew, while the truck cools down. Then as slow as I came up, I start going down. This is where it can be even more dangerous. Keep using your brakes and you end up without any, and you get to the bottom quicker than you expect. Use your gears and exhaust brake, and don't worry about them behind you.

At the bottom, it's an easy drive to the check point on the T junction at Tarsus. Here I make a quick brew before going on to Oryx at Adana. A BP diesel filling station come truck stop. Here you find out if you have a flat tyre before you even pull in. The kids can smell a blow out and know what wheel. The market/bazaar where you can buy anything, and I used to restock with fresh veg from. Then there is the NATO air base at the end of the bazaar street . shower and change of clothes then a couple of beers before a few of us make a camion stew. That's where you get whatever food you have and you just add it to the pot. Well we had four large pots on the go. There was stewing beef, chicken bits, pork, lamb, or then again it could have been goat. Potatoes, carrots, something that looked like sweed, and cabbage. All in a thick gravy, and spiced up with chillies and fresh spices from the market. Everyone was invited, all they had to do was bring the four of us a beer each and their plate and tuck in. All together there were about thirty of us. And come the morning there were four of us still there at midday. Did we ever put some beer away. So that day was cancelled. It was spent sitting in Oryx's shop drinking iced lemon tea.

Another day, and a few more miles, there's now four of us running together. As we pull in at the check point at Gaziantep, the police pull in from the other direction. And tell us that we must stay until the road has been cleared. A big accident at the bottom of a hill after the tunnel. Two kamikaze coaches and three trucks, all Hungarian. But many dead Turkish people. Well we all know who will get the blame for this. The Hungarian truck drivers will. If they had not been in Turkey the accident would not have happened. And those truckers were in for the hiding of their lives, by the Turkish police and locals. We all felt sorry for them as there was nothing that we could say or do to help them. It was 3am the next morning that they banged on our cabs to tell us to go . the road was open again. As we went past where the accident had been there was no sign of the coaches, but the three trucks were there and we could see that they had been looted by the Turks, as the cab doors were open, and the sheets from the trailers were laying out in the fields, where they had been pulled off, and there were people still there as well, but no police in sight. It was getting hot as we pulled in at Urfa check point so we all decided to stop down the road by the river. And have a dip. Good job we kept our Y fronts on as we soon had a few women and girls giggling on the bank. We drove away from there still in only our Y fronts and waving back to the women as we went.

We made it just past the big military base at Kiziltepe and pulled in at a truck parking area just before the wire fence around this country marks the Syrian border. It's the same as the communist iron curtain, watch towers as well, this should be our last night in Turkey. As from here we can make it to Zakho the Iraq border. And we leave here before the sun is up and head for the last check point at Cizre. I could never make out why as you came into this hell hole of a town, the last quarter of the hill, and all the way through the town, the road was marked out by one foot high kerb stones. But there was no road, only a pot holed dirt track that was about fifteen foot wide. The tarmac stopped and re started at the kerb stones each end of the town. And you could always tell when you were near the town. The stench. No sewerage works ever smelt like this town. You drove through with your windows shut and all your air vents shut, for the stench. And your screen wipers on for the fly's, mind they were everywhere. We are now in what the Turks and Kurds call Kurdistan. Now you are in bandit country. These men walk around with rifles slung over their shoulders, and swords hanging from their belts. And they are not afraid to use them, as the Turk army will tell you. Some of them even show off the souvenirs that they have taken from the Turks.

All along the side of the road the Kurdish kids would be there selling blocks of ice, cans of coke, and fruit. And scrounging cigs from you. All the way to Zakho, the Iraq border. We were about twenty Km from the border when we pulled up at the rear of the queue. First thing was that the kettle went on for a brew. By the time you had done that you had about six or eight of these kids hanging on your truck, all trying to sell something or after cigs. The older ones would come up and try to be the big I am, and chase the little ones off, then he would try and get you to buy something. He would even try and sell you his sister who would be standing there next to him. Or he was the big man changing money. Turk Lire, D Mark or English pounds into Iraqi Dinar, on the black market. Mind it was a good rate. Normally they would leave you after about half an hour or if more trucks pulled up behind you. But there would be another group of them a couple of hundred yards up the road, and so it went on.

We took it in turns to brew up and wake each other up as the queue moved forward a couple of truck lengths at a time. Only fridge and livestock trucks never queued up but went to the front, and as at Kapikula. There was Young Turk. His runner would be walking up and down the road looking for the Brits in the last Km as he could get your paperwork done by the time you arrived opposite his office. But it had taken us eight hours to meet up with the lad, and another two to get to his office and its now 2am as we pay him and head for the bridge over the Tigris into Iraq. There is only two trucks between us four and the border, when the Turks decide to strike. That's it. This could be two hours or two weeks, no telling. All we can do is sit and wait. So bloody close to getting out of this flea ridden country.

Flamingos on salt flats.

Top Deck. All set for another trip.

The two great Mosques of Istanbul

The old Roman bridge at Adana

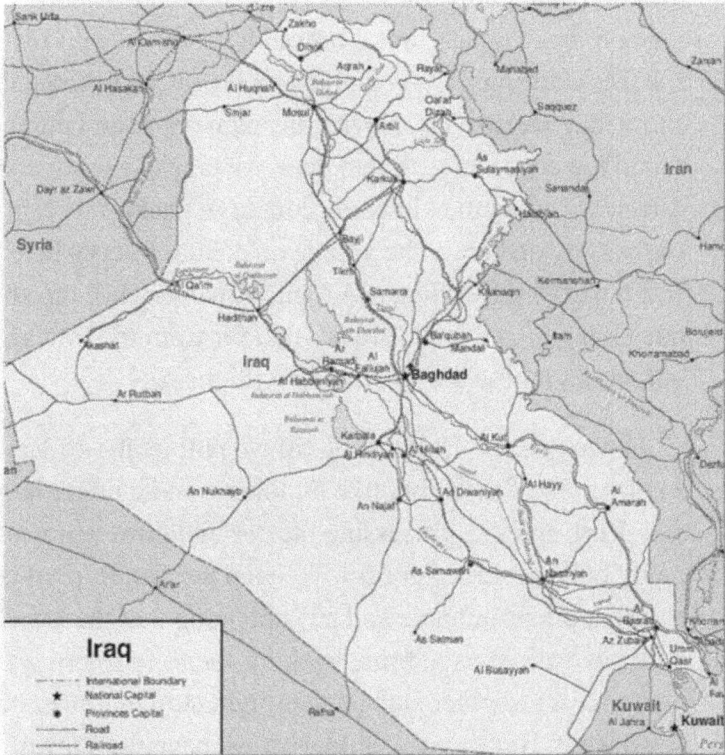

THE BIRTH PLACE OF CIVILISATION.

At 8am the border is open again and we are over the river that feeds the Tigris and in Iraq. The guard only looks at our trucks and waves us over to the parking area these people love the Brits, and we are given priority treatment through customs. Called to the front of any queue, no matter how long it is. We are done in half an hour, and can go when we please. But we have to follow tradition, and go over and have a glass of chi with the old man on the exit gate first. This old boy was a scout for the L.R.D.G. during WW2, and is proud of it, as his medals show that they are his. Having his name rank and number round the edge. So with that done we take our leave and drive out giving the old boy a couple of packets of cigs as we pass by and enter the village of Zakho. Everywhere you look there is military. AA guns on every hill top and machine gun nests. We are not that far from the Iranian border, and these are still at war with them.

Down past Da Huk and on till we pull in at Tafl Kayf, a collection of small hut like buildings, and a rather large new Ross chicken processing factory and farm that's being built by a British firm. We stop here to drop off old newspapers from home and any shopping that the lads here have asked us to bring back for them. In return we get to have a shower and an overnight stop in proper beds if we want. But its only midday so we have the shower and a chat as we have a good cup of coffee before moving off. We each grab a couple of broken pallets and thigh them onto our trailers before we go for the fire at Fallujah.

Within a few miles we are on the new highway to Baghdad, and can now make a bit of time up, so its pedal to the metal time as we race past Mawsil and Tikrit. We make one stop for a brew at Samarra. It's starting to get dark as we leave and head down for Baghdad. That's one thing out here it gets dark quick, and now with all lights on and not as fast. You tend to be more watchful at night, as your main worry is the camel. These stupid animals tend to lay down and sleep on the road, as the tarmac holds the heat. And you can bet your life that you could hit the most mangy looking camel and find out that it is a thorough bread champion and worth thousands.

We reach the military radio station and swing right, past the prison and the army driving school. And pull in at the fuel point to get our 200 Lt, get the trip tick marked and off we go again up the road to Fallujah. The first thing you see is the glow from the fire then the lights of the customs post as you come into the town. Round the roundabout and back on yourself. Past the customs, then turn right onto the track leading out into the desert just past the trucks and fire, then right again at the tyres and head for the fire . drive round the back of the trucks pulling into any gap you can get into. There is a rule here that all new drivers, that is those that have just arrived, get the beer out. Lucky for us there are four of us, as at times it can be costly. There are normally between fifteen and twenty five Brits here waiting for customs or the tanker. One of the drivers tells us that there is still some chicken and bread left if want to help ourselves.

The sun is up and so am I. There's no one about so I make myself a coffee, grab my papers and head of towards the customs. Prat. Its Friday, nothing will get done today. It would be like asking the Pope to work on Sunday. It's the Muslim holy day. About turn and back to the truck, before anyone sees me. Put the papers back and grab my wash kit and head off back to the customs to use the wash, and fill up my water bottles. Back at the trucks someone has the kettle on and there's tea and coffee on the go. I open one of my trailer boxes and get the cooker and frying pans out, one for the eggs and one for the bacon. That will soon drag them out of their cabs. Problem is it also wakes the others. The Dutch and Danes and the Germans, but they all contribute and we all get along. Case of having to. We are all a long way from home. The day is spent servicing the trucks and trailers, changing and replacing tyres. Not the best place to do this but it has to be done.

Saturday early morning and we are over at the customs, hand our papers in and register with land transport. Round to Davies Turners office and see this lazy Brit about getting a fax back to Mavertons and a call home to Joan. That he can do, the fax well that may take a while, so I grab the phone and as normal you have to book the call. Give the operator the number you want and the number you are calling from and they will call you at a set time. You have to give Saddams police time to set up. Write the fax to Lou, Johnnie , and Bert to let them know that I am here and to send any instructions here. Phone rings, my call to Joan, great I hear her, and we both hear them pick up.

After lunch we are back at customs to find out if we are clear and able to go and deliver our cargo. My load is Military. It's a generator. And I have to deliver it tomorrow. There is an official letter for me with my instructions. Go to cross roads in village of Al Batha, south of Samawa and wait for army escort tomorrow morning to guide me to As Salman. The customs say that I have to go now to be there for the morning early the oasis of As Salman is in the Muthanna desert and very hot there. It's hot everywhere, the only time it gets below +50c is at night this time of year.

Back at the trucks those that are clear are getting set to go. A look at my old map. Yer it's an all afternoon and night run to this Al Batha place. Just hope I find the cross roads. Looks like a track to this oasis. My first stop is the fuel point to get 200 Lt of diesel. At first he is not going to give me any as I have only been sitting at Fallujah that is till I show him the Military letter, and he fills both my tanks. Not going to complain, and he don't want paying. On a winner here. Round Baghdad and out on the Basrah highway. I make it to Babylon and stop for break. From the highway you can see the ruins of the old city. In good condition and looked after. I have been round it and you are not allowed to touch anything as it still being researched by British and Iraqis. I am not even at Samawa, and it is getting dark. I turn all my lights on, its daylight now. That's six halogen spots on the roof, head lights, and four halogen spots above the bumper, there's no chance of missing the turn off now.

If I hadn't had all my lights on I would have missed Al Batha. Six small huts and a truck wash. And there's the track with a small notice board pointing out the direction to As Salman. Park up and get the kettle on, then get a few hours sleep. It seems like I have only just gone to sleep, and I am being woken up. It's just starting to get light, and there's an army land rover with an officer and a couple of soldiers. Don't even get a chance to make a brew, as they want to be on their way. The track aint bad at first, then after about a mile it don't exist. All there is, is every hundred yards is an old oil drum painted red, or there's a pile of rocks to mark the track. We, well I am managing to do 10/15 MPH max with this load. And the officer in the land rover keeps waving for me to keep up. Two hours later we reach the oasis, and there's no one there. Everyone has gone, and the officer is on the radio. Now I get the good news. We have now to go another couple of hours to a place called Takhadid and it is out in the Hijarah or Iraq's Sahara. This place is not meant for artics. We finally arrive in the middle of nowhere to find a whole tank regiment and an infantry regiment. The thing is this lot have brand new Chieftain battle tanks. British. They have just got the generator off when its panic stations. Everyone is turning vehicles round to face away from the wind that has just started and is getting stronger, then I see it a sand storm, and there is a deep red cloud heading towards us. I jack knife the truck round and close everything down. All you can do is ride it out, as long as it takes. Kettle on and a brew I think.

An hour later it had gone, so had the markers for the track. I just hope that someone here knows the way back to Samawa. They found someone. A ten year old Bedouin lad. No problem keeping up with him on his camel. That animal had it right, who want to rush around in this heat. When we got to the oasis at As Salman we stopped. His family had set up their camp. And I was invited to stop the night and eat with them. We would go on in the morning. This was going to be interesting, I only knew about a dozen words of Arabic. The head man knew a fair bit of English, and between us we got through and I had a great night with them. And the meal was fantastic. Don't know what it was, but everything was fresh. All the fruit and the veg. The meat I think was goat. But it was great then ice cold water to rinse our mouths and sweet hot chi, I was a bit of a novelty for his younger daughters, they had never seen a westerner even with my tan I was still pale to them. The one thing that I noticed was his family were not strict Muslims. The women still served the men first but they ate with the men not separate. Everything was eaten with your fingers or knife and you only used your right hand and the last prayer of the day was said at sunset, but I took my leave before then and went to bed. In the morning I was awakened with a glass of chi by the eldest daughter. Then the young lad came over with his camel and he was joined by the rest of the family to see me off. When we got to the highway at Samawa I gave him four packets of cigs, and a small mirror for him to give to his sisters. And before he could argue I pulled out and headed north for Baghdad and Fallujah. I stopped again at Babylon for a break. There is so much history in this country and part of the world. I love the desert and its people.

The evening meal was just about ready as I pulled into the parking area at Fallujah and dumped the timbers from my load down by the fire. That was another thing, in the 12 years that I did this run to the middle east and gulf states. I have never known that fire to be out. One of the lads had a message for me from D.Ts man. I had to go and see him first thing in the morning as he had urgent instructions from Mavertons. But whatever they were I for one was going to have a couple of beers up at the chicken shop. Tomorrow would take care of itself. No one fancied the walk over there so I went on my own. Four cans of Heineken later I walked back followed by a donkey who was collected a few minutes later by a very happy old Iraqi that I had been drinking with

Tomorrow came and I was sitting outside D.Ts office , up by the customs drinking a hot coffee, waiting for the agent to arrive. When he arrived and we went into his office, he looked at me and smiled. Anyone else had done that would have been picking themselves up off the floor. He handed me the fax and started to laugh. The air went blue. Not a lot of ABC. Nearly all F.B.C. "They want me to do what." "He's F***in where?" "Another F***in subby, that can't do the job." "Cant he tell the difference between IRAQ and F***in IRAN?" That is a short version of what was said. And all D.Ts man could say between the laughter was, "I take it you're not impressed smurf." That was putting it mildly. O. K I had bluffed my way onto Mavertons, never having been out here before. But I was never afraid to ask if I didn't know anything. Not like these subby. Owner drivers, all they see is the money, not what they have to do to earn it, then they bottle out, leaving us, the drivers that work for the companies to pick up their mess and sort them out, as they just haven't got a clue.

This F***in prize prat, has one of our low loaders behind him with a D 9 Caterpillar Bulldozer on destined for Basrah Iraq. This prat is at DOGUBAYAZIT. North east Turkey. The border with IRAN. To say that he has fucked up big time is about right. And for once I am in agreement with the Turks. His TIR control sheet is blank.

He has not got one stamp or signature on it after Kapikula. He has entered the customs post and handed his paperwork over. The customs there have cancelled it and now new paperwork is required to get the load from there to Iraq. Plus there's a F in great fine to pay. And there at the bottom of the fax is the sweetener. It's worth another £500 to me if I sort it. D.Ts lad must have already booked the call. Lou Sains is on the phone. "you calmed down smurf". Then he starts telling me what he is going to do at his end, and what he wants me to do this end. Then I tell him what I am going to do. And that is I am going to take the low loader from him and get him the fuck out of it with my empty trailer, and I will do the job but I want more than just the £500 for doing it, I am also going to need full trip running money as there are a few palms that are going to need greasing. From here to Ankara and out to him, then back down to here and Basrah. "good lad smurf, just what I wanted you to say, all set up at this end. Paperwork is DHL to Ankara airport everything in your name and waiting for you to collect it, and the money is at Western union at the airport as well. So what you doing talking to me. Move it mate." And the phone goes dead as he hangs up.

Time for a beer. Up to the chicken shop, half a chicken, and a few cans of Heineken to take back to the truck. Everyone has a smile on their face. He has been and in broad daylight. The tanker. He came in off the desert and parked at the back of every one and filled all our belly tanks using a small long hose. I owed one of the lads 10 D Mark. How if my belly tank was full he had to have put about eight hundred Lt in it. Still I wasn't going to argue,

I gave the lad his money. The tanker had been to the park before, but not in daylight. That was risky for all. When I went back in the afternoon to get my empty papers and land transport papers, it seemed as if all the customs knew what I was going to do. And all wanted to shake my hand. As they all thought that I was crazy. Mind you so did I. With all my papers back, stamped and signed, it's time for me to head off up the road and sort out that prat. I am only going to stop at the Ross factory, so its foot down all the way. The Brits have just finished work as I pull up out by the gate and climb out of the cab. I ask if I can just have a quick shower and a coffee, and tell them what I am doing, so there's not a lot that I can bring back.

At 2am one of the lads wakes me up as I have crashed out on their sofa, and want to go into the border early and with a bit of luck miss the diesel check. Through Da Huk, and Zakho, past the diesel check point before they realise that I am there, and in through the customs gate. Ten minutes and I am on my way over the Bridge and into Turkey again. Park and go over to Young Turks office. And explain to him that I want a TIR control paper to Dogubayazit, empty. Half an hour later the papers are done and I am on my way. From here on its only going to be coffee breaks, and a couple of hours sleep to Adana, before going up and over tarsus to Ankara. Through Cizre, up the hill and pull over for a break. Kiziltepe, another break and a bacon sandwich, only the bacon looks a funny colour, so I make do with corned beef. I think that's what it is. It looks and tastes alright. A couple of hours kip and I am on my way again, nonstop now to Gaziantep, as I go through Urfa check point there's another one of our subby asleep. On I go, and by the time I pull in at the check point at Gaziantep I am in need of some sleep. Paper done first then a coffee and crash out on top of the bunk. Four hours later I am awakened by a Brit who wants to know if I want a brew. He was lucky, as he was an old mate he got the,"hi mate what you doing". And not the F.O and let me sleep. Coffee and a chat then we part company, and I head for Oryx's at Adana, a shower, meal and a few more hours kip. As I pull in and park, its 38 hours since I left the lads at the Ross factory back at Tafl Kayf, and I look and feel like shit. It's time for a change of clothes and a shower and shave, followed by a meal then bed till whenever I wake up. As the next leg is also going to be nonstop to Ankara.

Midnight and I am awake. That's a good six hours sleep. A quick wash to freshen up, and a couple of cups of coffee and I am ready for the off. I should be up and over the mountain before daybreak. Didn't make it over, but did see the sun rise from the top as I made a coffee, then went down and I did manage to get through Aksaray before midday and parked up for a break at the ruins on the salt flats, with a couple of Danes who were just getting up and had the coffee on the go. I spent an hour with them, then headed north and onto Ankara and the Telex Motel. They had just started the evening meal as I pulled in and parked up. Not many here, only eight trucks, mainly Dutch and Danes, and one other Brit who was sitting in his cab having a brew. Another first timer. And he was pulling for us. And he was waiting for me to arrive. He had a Telex from Johnny Spiller telling him to wait there for me. As I would take him through to

Baghdad. When I asked him why he wasn't inside having a meal or a beer, his answer was that there were no other Brits here yet. So I told him that the Dutch and Danes spoke to each other in English, so he had nothing to worry about. He finished his coffee and we both went upstairs to the bar and joined the other idiots. He knew about the other driver and said that he was not an owner driver, but worked for the same firm as he did. Only when he gets back he is sacked, but not to say anything if he sees him. So I tell him he has a choice. Stay here and wait for me to come back. Or lock his truck up and come with me. That way he will see a bit more of Turkey, and he will not be spending money on booze. But in the morning I have a bit of running around to do, so if he wants he can come with me. I have the airport to do and I want some info from the police, so I have to find their head quarters.

The airport was easy to get to but to get to freight terminal and DHL was another matter. I got the package with the paperwork, then had to find Western union. Airport terminals are not the best places to try out your truck driving skills, even if you are solo. That is no trailer. A few slagging matches with the taxi drivers and I park or rather abandon it in the end and walk in to find it. By the time I have found it had another ruck with them and demanded the money in US Dollars as it was paid in to their office in London. And then got back to find that the truck had a few parking tickets on it. That I tore up and handed back to this traffic warden or whatever and drove away back to the city. Now to find the old bill shop. I can see it, a ruddy great radio mast on its roof. Getting there is not so easy. I had past this cop about four times, when he stops me and in perfect English ask if I am lost. Me lost, never. Just I could not find the way to where I wanted to get to. Not lost.

The police are very helpful. I only have two questions for them. 1 can I go from Dogubayazit to Zakho via Elazig and Diyarbakir?, yes if I get the TIR control paper from the border. 2 can I get the TIR control paper for my friends truck changed so that he can come with me? No his route is to Zakho already but I can go solo and not require a control paper. Can I have that I writing please? No problem. That all sorted, its back to the Telex and a few beers. But I have a plan. Phone Young Turk at the border and find out from him. I don't fancy going all the way there then all the way back, when there is a shorter route down to Zakho, and if he can get it sorted for us if we pay the customs at the border and him. Give him the number of the Telex and wait for him to call back. Two hours later he is back on the phone and has the chief customs officer there. It's all sorted. I must pay 100 dollar fine for truck now in compound. 50 dollar new control paper for me to take trailer. 100 dollar for friend to get new control paper. 10 dollar to each control from Ankara. Plus Young Turks fee. Paying all that was still working out cheaper, and shorter in time as well. All I said to him was "see you in four days Arbi".

Early the next morning I wake the other lad and tell him to grab a change of clothes and his wash kit. I have changed my mind, we will take my truck to the border. We can be back here inside a week and Iraq in two. So it's a quick wash and a coffee, and we are on our way. I pass

him an old map of Turkey and tell him our route from
Ankara. Its nearly a straight line east to the border. First
place is Kirikkate then Sivas and Erzurum. And into
Dogubayazit the border with Iran. But between Erzurum
and the border he will see a very holy mountain, that is
mentioned in the old testament of the bible. Mount Ararat.
Where Noah's Ark came to land at the end of the great
flood. People still go up the mountain looking for bits of
the ark. How they are going to find anything is beyond
me, as the mountain is snow covered all year, and it is a
dormant volcano biding its time to erupt.

Mount Ararat from near the border with Iran.

We made Sivas that day and parked with a couple of Dutch lads on Breda transport, had a brew and a couple of sandwiches and turned in for a few hours kip. It was still dark as I got up and started towards Erzurum. Up into the mountains of northern Turkey. Now this was where you did find the bandits. They were from northern Iran, Armenia, and Georgia. (Russia then) As well as the locals. The kids were the worst, I used to hate the little gits. They used to stand by the side of the road calling out for cigs, and if you didn't give them you got a rock in your side window or your windscreen. But I had my own little frightener. A sawn off shot gun. I used to pick it up and leave it with Young Turk, coming in and going out of the country at either border. All the agents used to keep them for the European drivers. Just seeing the barrels was enough for the kids to back off and some of the men. And as for the stories of getting shot up by bandits, that's what they were Stories. I never saw a truck with a bullet hole. Plenty with smashed windows and screens. Our second stop was Erzurum with another Brit on his way home. Driving for Eric Vick. One of the first Brit firms to come out here. He had seen the driver that we were on our way to, and said that the lad was about to drop the trailer and go back to Istanbul and fly home. How he was going to do that no one knew. But he thought he had talked him into waiting for us to get there as Young Turk said he had spoken to us. Right early the next day I am up and away. I aint stopping now till I get to the border and find this clown. I want to get turned round and on our way back before dark. What he does after I have swapped trailers I don't care. If he is already thinking of abandoning the rig, he can do it after I have gone.

I hit a pot hole and my passenger falls out of the top bunk. Asks where we are? I don't know not far from the border. About another hour or so. Then he asks if we are stopping before there, and I tell him only to blow fuel from the trailer into the truck tanks while he puts the kettle on for a quick brew. And when we get to the border and I turn round. I want him to uncouple and drop this trailer, while I get the paperwork for the other one sorted. There's the other trailer already dropped and there's the unit. I swing round and park alongside. We both go over to Young Turks office with the new paperwork and new TIR carnet. The agent does not look very happy. There is a problem. Not with the paperwork, he just needs it now to get stamped and we will be away after we have paid the fine and other money. The problem is, when he opened the office this morning there was a letter and the keys to the truck. The driver has gone in the night. What about the truck. No problem, the lad that has come with me can drive it back to Ankara.

We have just finished coupling the trailers when Young Turks lad comes over with the customs chief and all the paperwork done. I just have to pay the man and check that it is all there. And that the TIR control paper is from here to Zakho via Ankara. And one from here to Ankara for the other truck and an empty paper, all done we shake hands and I part with 200 dollars and two packets of cigs. The chief is happy and Young Turk is happy as I give him 50 dollars, and we climb into the trucks and pull away from the customs, heading back to Erzurum and a kip. There will be no racing with this load on. Its late and dark as we come into the town and find some where to park up alongside each other for the night. It looks like the driver only took his clothes and left everything else. So we made use of his cooker and brew kit. Under the bunk there was enough tinned food to last a month. I told the lad that we would share everything out that he had left when we got back to Ankara.

It took three days to get back to the Telex, as I had two blow outs on the low loader and now I had no spares. This King trailer had 16 tyres, that's four axels and all steer. But the prat who brought it down had the axels locked and had scrubbed every tyre nearly bald. That meant that I was going to need all 16 replacing before we left here, and that meant more F in money to spend on this load. Mavertons were not going to be happy when I phone in.

Bert Worth went through the roof when I told him about the tyres and the driver doing a bunk. Then I heard Lou say tell him to flog the truck and trailer.. we will keep the low loader. Then he came on himself. "sell the F in lot smurf, do what you got to do and get it done mate. That prats card is well marked, we will take care of him, and call me from Baghdad, see ya."

Three days later I am 3500 dollars and 16 tyres better off, and I have managed to salvage four of the old tyres that will do as spares for now. And there's a Turk haulier that now has a Scania 140 and a 40ft super cube trailer, with a belly tank that runs the length of the floor up between the chassis and a young Brit trucker that has more gear than what he started with. A good meal and a good night's sleep. Ready to start the trip again. Both our tanks are full from draining the belly tank of the trailer I sold we are ready to roll.

The roof of my truck is getting a bit cluttered with lights. Six spots two round amber flashing lights, and now the flashing light bar from the other truck. All the marker lights down the trailer and on the back. I am lit up like a Christmas tree, as we pull out of the Telex at four in the morning heading for the Taurus mountains and our first stop at the salt flats, where the lad gets his first sight of wild flamingos by the hundreds. We spend an hour here having a brew and a sandwich before moving off again . through Aksaray and onto the foothills of the mountains where we park for the night, or rather till the early hours. Sooner he went over in the dark while there is little traffic and he can't see how high he is over the side of the mountain. He can do what he wants on the way back empty, and I aint around.

Its midnight as I give him a shout, the kettle is boiling and the coffee is about ready. I will keep the flashing lights off unless I see traffic coming towards us, and for him to stay close. And that there is a stop at the top at the control point, where we let the trucks cool down and we have a brew. With that we are away. Two hours later we are pulling in at the top and all my lights are flashing. Just for the cops. An hour later we are on our down to Tarsus and Adana. Into Oryx and in the parking area, its breakfast time. Eight o, clock and everyone has gone the place is empty. Check the cat and all the chains are still tight and all the tyres. I am also going to change the oil and fuel filters while we are here, there isn't anywhere really after here till you get to Fallujah, and that's not the best environment to do services in with all the sand. Midday and we are pulling out. Restocked with fruit and veg ice in the cool box, I intend to make Gaziantep for the night. There's a big bit of open ground opposite the Hotel. We can get a meal in there and a beer. May as well show the lad some of the better places to stop out here.

It's just getting light as we pull away up the hill and through the tunnel. Now I send the lad through first and for him to sound his horns when he is through and he has stopped the traffic by putting himself across both lanes so that I can come through down the middle of the road. I am three quarters of the way through with all my lights flashing, and here comes a kamikaze coach. Couldn't wait went round three trucks and four cars. Now the idiot thinks I am going to move out of his way. No chance pal. I keep getting closer to him. He gets out of the coach waving his arms about and has a steel bar in his hand. That's it I stop and get out of the cab, only I have a Purdy double barrel in my hands. That's changed his mind, he's back in the coach and going backwards at speed. As I come out and past him I take his side mirror with the cat just for good measure.

Through Urfa and onto Kiziltepe and a few hours sleep. I tell him that we will be running alongside the Syrian border and that we are about to enter Kurdistan in the morning and also to keep his windows shut as we go through Cizre because of the smell and fly's. We are parked just past the army barracks, and in the middle of the night the whole garrison must have decided to move out. For about an hour there were trucks and armoured vehicles going past us. So I put the kettle on and had a brew. Gave them a bit longer to get where ever they were going, and we set of as well, and got through Cizre before the locals were up and about. Where the traffic was I don't know but we never hit the queue till we were about a mile from the border. There were only about half a dozen Kurdish lads about selling coca cola and ice, and only two doing the money change. Young Turks lad found us, and told us to pull round the trucks in front as they all had big problems with Turkish police. We were now at the front of the queue, with only a Dutch truck in front down by the bridge. And he seemed to be having words with the border guard. He was still there when we were waved round him and across the bridge into Iraq.

Zakho customs and its empty. Show passports to the guard and park up near the exit gate. Get all our paperwork and go into the customs hall, no one about, so I go over o the door in the far corner, knock and walk in. They are all in here having chi and a smoke. "hello mister nargi, you have chi, your friend also I do papers." As one of the older customs men gets up and takes our papers and shakes my hand. When he comes back in with the papers. He tells the lad that he has to go to Haswa Terminal and unload in shed 1, Military shed. Not to go to customs at Fallujah, he has done it here, and he will get signed up and empty paper there also. Me I must go sit at Fallujah, then go long way to Basrah. And get empty paper when I come back to Fallujah. They all think it's funny and start laughing. With that I say my good byes and go back to the truck. It's just starting to get light as we pull out.

With a good run we should make Fallujah by about tea time tonight. There is no sign of life yet at the Ross factory as we drive past, and stop near Mawsil for a break. There is a lot of military about today, and all heading out towards Kirkuk, that means there's something going on over near Solaymaniyah and the Iranian border. We stop just past Samarra for our last break, and a meal of ham and eggs. We are still about twenty miles from Baghdad, when we hear a couple of dull explosions and can just see smoke in the distance. Missile strikes. Best if we make a move and get to Fallujah quick this road is going to get a bit busy soon, with troop movement, as is Baghdad.

As we come into Baghdad it looks like the Ayatollah was aiming for the radio masts, and missed. Hitting the milk bottling plant instead, and part of the local school. I pull over and park. Grab my first aid kit and go and help. The other lad does the same. Men and women and kids are just wandering about in a daze covered in blood and bust. We do what we can for them, with what we have. Doctors from the hospitals arrive along with nurses. A lot of these are British and Irish girls, as are the doctors. They thank us both for helping out and tell us that we can carry on as they will take over with the military rescue teams.

We are soon at Fallujah, and parked up on the desert with a few of the other lads. Some of them have gone off with the tanker driver. He turned up just as the missiles landed. I told them that there would not be any fresh milk for a while, as we told them what had happened back down the road. One of Astrans drivers put the brew on and we went and sat around his truck, waiting for the others to come back, before we started to make the evening meal. We didn't have to wait long before they started pulling in, and telling us how they got away without being spotted by the Army while they were filling up from the tanker, and again on their way back here off the desert. Apparently the area was crawling with military and police.

Just after midnight two army Land Rovers pulled into the parking area along with a police car. An English doctor got out and asked for the drive with the Caterpillar. They needed me to come and clear some of the buildings with the cat. The rest of the lads said that they also wanted to help. In the end we even got the East European drivers to come and help, in all there was about thirty drivers there. And we worked all through the night. As for me with the caterpillar. I hadn't driven a tracked vehicle since the army, and then it was a 432 APC. Not a lot of difference, steering was the same with the levers, just that I had to figure out the blade controls. In the end it was getting off, and back on the trailer that was the hard part. For helping out the army took me into the fuel depot at Haswa terminal and filled my truck and the cat up with diesel.

It was midmorning by the time we got back to Fallujah, and all we wanted to do was get cleaned up and our heads down for a bit of kip. But I wanted to be away first thing tomorrow and needed to get clear of customs today, and give the caterpillar a bit of a wash down before I get to Basrah. Nothing I could do about the paint work though. At least I can tell them it works properly. I put my papers in and register with land transport. One of the customs asks why we did not put our papers in this morning, now is too late to clear customs we will have to wait till tomorrow. So I ask him where he was all last night. As all us truck drivers were down the road digging out children and only finished this morning. And walked off leaving them looking at us. An hour later three of them came over to the trucks with all our papers done. Every one of us was clear to go and deliver, or home as even the empty papers were done.

Within half an hour most of the trucks had gone, and we waited for the dust and sand to settle before we could put the brew on. The first kettle had just boiled as the first new inbound truck pulled into the parking area. More timber and old tyres got put on the heap for the fire, and a couple of cookers were got out ready for tonight's meal, of whatever, or camion stew. That would be washed down with whatever beer we had left or wine. Only I was not going to stay up half the night drinking. I wanted to be away early in the morning, as I had a full days hard drive down to Basrah and the site where I was to deliver this cat to. So after the meal and a couple of beers I turned in for the night, leaving the lad in the hands of the other lads, knowing that apart from leading him astray, they would see that he was unloaded and looked after. Even get some one that was going back for him to tag onto after he had got his papers back. I just made sure that he had enough cash to get back with then turned in for the night.

I was pulling of the desert just as the old boy started calling everyone to prayer. It was sun rise. As I pulled out onto the road I put all my flashing light on and headed for the Baghdad ring and the Basrah highway. There are two ways to get there, one is by the top road going via Kut and Ammarah, along the river Tigris. Or the bottom road that I and all the others favour. It may not be as wide, but it didn't go via the mosquito infested marshes and lakes. And it wasn't long before I was stopping for a break at Hellah. Then another easy drive to Diwaniyah and Samawa. Here I pick up the river Euphrates and pull in for diesel and a break at a small hut on the side of the road serving ice cold lemon and coke, there's also a truck wash. I get the lads there to give the cat a quick wash while I have a break. Only they go and wash the lot, cat, trailer and truck. Pay for the drink, then go and haggle over the cost of the wash, in the end I settle for two Dinar and two packets of cigs. From here I follow the river to Naseriyeh. This is where the new road from Basrah is coming to. What the cat I have is going to help build. I still have just about 220 Km to go and its mid afternoon as still following the river over to Al Quanah where the Tigris and the Euphrates meet and turn into the Shatt Al Arab canal all the way past Basrah to the Gulf. Only at a small village in Iran called Shaliamoneh the canal changes sides and leaves Iraq and is controlled by the Iranians, who have two of their big military bases at Khorramshar, and Abadan. It's getting dark as I come up to Basrah airport and go on towards the city. Now I need the highway to Kuwait. Now it is dark and I need to find the site. In the end I give up and pull up at one of the all night truck stops that are everywhere on this road. Brew and kip. That's all I want now.

Just got parked up, where I am under the lights and where I can get out in the morning, when this Land Cruiser pulls up alongside me. Only he is shouting at the wrong side of the truck. It may be Brit but this is a left hand drive, and I am not in the truck but round the other side having a brew. Leave him long enough and he will figure it out for himself. An Arab driver tells him that I am on the other side of the truck talking to a Jordanian driver who is parked next to me.

No hello, hi Yer mate. But "where the fuck have you been, you should have been here two weeks ago". And knocks the coffee out of my cup and all over the Jordanian driver, as he gives me shove. Next thing he is on his back, and a size 9 rigger boot is screwing hell out of his balls. That's when a few of his mates start coming over the road, and about twenty Arab drivers stand in their way. I let him up and tell him he is lucky that the cat is here and not in Tehran, and if he starts again in the morning when I drive it off the trailer, I may just put it on top of him, and to F O before these lads have a go, and to apologise to the Jordanian for the coffee.

Its nine o'clock and I get out of the truck and walk round, there on the other side of the road about 200 yards down is the site, and I can see a couple of the Brits wandering about near the gate looking over at me waiting.

Then a car pulls in and parks in front of the truck and a bloke in shirt and tie gets out and comes towards me. This prat has the same attitude as the last one. He starts poking me, telling me that I am costing them money, by being late and to get my arss in gear. That it, one into his fat gut and knee into his nose as he doubles over. Get in the truck and push the car sideways into the storm drain. Now to deliver the cat. There are two Iraqi police cars sitting on the truck park and the four cops are just sitting there watching, doing nothing. I drive down the road and turn round and come back up the dual carriageway, off at the slip road to the site not even slowing down. The Brits have seen me coming and know what's going to happen, and rush to open the gates. Only I drive in the first gates they are only just open. This is their living compound and not the work compound. Sorry, a big U turn sending dust and everything up in the air. Into their quarters where their wives were and into their swimming pool. Then I went into the work compound and spun the truck round and up to the gate. No one said a word. I was out of the truck, chains off and up the front of the trailer. Ramps down, and drove the cat off. Put the ramps up, and then got one of the Brits to sign for it and I made him get the company stamp as well. While he was off doing that I drained all the fuel out of the cat and into my truck. If that was Kier French they could stuff their selves. They had pissed me right off.

As I drove away back towards Basrah, there was one of their 4x4s trying to get the car out of the storm drain, and matey with the shirt and tie was with the police pointing at me and doing his nut. The cops were not interested, there was no Iraqi involved. And I got back to Naseriyeh before stopping for a break. I was really wound up by them prats and needed to cool off. And about 40 Km up the road was a pull in with a cold drinks hut, and behind that was a small river I was going for a dip as well as a break. I only made it to Hilla that day, and by the time I had made a brew and something to eat I had calmed down and having a laugh about it. It would be a long time before they started on another drive again. But I knew that sooner or later they would be on the phone back to the UK, and that I would hear something a well.

I pulled onto the desert at midday at Fallujah, and went over to get my empty paper and see D.Ts man. "upset a few people did we smurf." That was his first words to me as I walked into his office. "they won't pick on me again in a hurry, will they." As I sat down and poured myself coffee. He handed me a paper, all in Arabic then gave me one in English. My reload, right out at Rutbah, towards Jordan. A military Westland helicopter going back to Westland's in England. And my route back was via Syria, Cyprus and Greece. I was not allowed through Turkey or the Eastern bloc countries. Great now I had to get ferries as well. Miss one and it could be up to a week till the next one. I hadn't been out long enough already on this trip.

The air base where I was to load this helicopter was well out of Rutbah on the road to Damascus, Syria. And they were expecting me there tomorrow midday, as they would have everything ready to lift it onto the low loader. I was also given a large brown envelope with all the paperwork in Arabic and English. The customs had been done. And all I had to do was go and load it. From Fallujah it was going to take the rest of this afternoon and a good part of the night to get there. But at least it was nearly a straight line, up to Ramadi and follow the highway out into the desert to Rutbah, and about ten Km the other side was the main road to Syria and Damascus. The Iraqi classed this highway along with the one down from Mosul to Hillah a motorway, all it was, was a tarmac road that was about four lanes wide, no centre reservation or hard shoulder. The odd fuel point on one side of the road , and every few miles there would be s small shack selling cold drinks, ice and fruit. And every now and then the odd camel laying in the roar at night. But by far the best thing out on these desert roads. Iraq, or Saudi was the chicken run at night. This was the Jordanian truckers, seeing just how brave they were, which wasn't very at all.

The way this was played out was, they would come down the road with their lights on and see yours coming towards them. So they would switch their lights off, then turn them back on when they were on your side of the road. That was when we would go to the other side, and they would cross back and turn them off again. And so did we, now no one has lights, and he would panic, next thing he had every light on and he would be pulling off onto the desert as you put yours back on and blasting away on the air horns as you went past him. These crazy stunts were pulled to keep you on your toes, in all the years I never saw two trucks crash, but I have seen a lot of cars that have tried the same thing against the Jordanian truckers and come off worse for it.

With the cooker set up in the centre of the cab and a full kettle of water and brew kit out, I didn't stop until reached the out skirts of Rutbah and pulled in off the road leaving my side lights on. I didn't want any tired out Syrian or Jordanian truck running into me. Time to cook a quick meal and get my head down for the night. It would only take me a couple of hours from here.

Round the tow and on to the split. Turn off the main highway and onto the road for Syria. This road is crawling with army. And as I get within sight of the base I come up to the first road block. I hand over a military movement order to one of the guards, he shows it to an officer who hands it back to me, has the barrier raised and tells a motor cyclist to escort me. He is gone like a bullet, so I just head for where I can see a crane next to a helicopter and a few people standing near it. I have one thing on my side here any way there are four people from Westland helicopters to oversee the loading. At least they should know how to do it. After four hours they have a cradle made and fixed to the trailer, for it to sit on. But there is one slight thing. The main top rotors are still fitted, and need to be taken off and packed down the side of the trailer. By the time this is done, and all that now has to be done is to lift it all onto my trailer. The crane driver and the Iraqi air force officers decide that it is too late and it will be done in the morning. The Westland lads all look at me, they can't believe it. So I have to tell them that here there is no such thing as time. Or as they say. Bukhara. Imshahla, tomorrow. God willing. With that I dropped the trailer where it was and took the truck backup to the top of the road to the split where I had seen a small Motel.

And booked myself in. As had the Brit lads. They had been here three days, but the first thing I needed was a shower, then a tomato salad and half a chicken. The lads were moaning about why they would not work till the morning. It's easy I said its now 11.30 and the sun is nearly overhead. The temperature is 44c and getting hotter. You go and work out there and see how long you last, but be up and ready at sunrise, as they will be as its cooler then. And we can get it loaded, chained down, and I can be parked up on the desert road between Sab Biyar and Homs in Syria for the night. Time for a couple of beers and a lay down by the pool and relax. An evening meal of roasted goat and cuscus with a tomato salad and a couple of glasses of Arak, and an early night.

By the time Westland's lads got to us, we had it loaded onto the trailer. I had all the papers signed and stamped by the Iraqi air force. They were just leaving as was the crane. Job done, all I was left with was to chain it all down. Sun rise was four hours ago, it's now nine, and starting to get a bit warm. Half an hour later I am over in the hanger having a shower, clean clothes,(shorts and T shirt) and a brew before going home.

Homeward Bound.

Everything chained down, and put away. It was time to roll, I was now on my way home. Turn left out of the base and 100 Km to the border at the village of At Tauf in Syria. When I pulled in at the customs they never said a word just looked at the load, stamped my papers and waved me through. I hadn't been in the country half an hour before a cop pulled me over wanting to know if I would give his mate a lift to Damascus. Sorry but I am turning off at Sab Biyar and going to Furqlus. No problem off he went, and an hour later I am at the split and turn right onto the small desert road. And just past the split I see the cops car. He is waiting to see if I did turn off or not. By the time I pull in at Furqlus, it's starting to get dark, so I pull well off the road leaving my side lights on, and get a meal and brew on the go.

It don't matter where in the world you go, there's going to be a Dutch man. And there he comes, right up to the front of my truck so we are looking at each other, and he is smiling as he gets his mug and comes over to me. Gives me his mug and says "Saturday mate, it's just gone." He knows that I am on my way to the ferry, now I have to wait three more days. No prob I will do the tourist bit tomorrow at Homs and the next day at Latakia. What's a few more days on this bloody trip anyway. At six the next morning this crazy Dutch man is waking me up with a mug of coffee. What do I want to be getting up at this stupid time for when I am no longer in any sort of rush. That day I had parked the truck outside Homs in a truck stop of sorts and got a taxi into the city to see some of the sights. Well he drove all over the place, pointing to this that and the other. I didn't know what he was on about, but there are a few interesting places, only he never stopped until we got to a big Mosque, right in the city. I managed to get one photo of it and when he saw me with the camera he said no photo we go quick. And we did, back to the truck. That past a few hours away, now for the last leg up to Latakia. Round Homs and along the highway that also forms and runs along the border with Lebanon, to the coast then up to Latakia along the coast. One look at the Med and I am looking for some where to park up for the night and tomorrow. Just outside of Baniyas a small fishing town on the coast I find a place just big enough to get well off the road, and a nice bit of beach to laze on for a day.

There is only so much beach you can take, and by mid afternoon I had my fill. So after a cup of coffee I moved off and went on to Latakia and into the ferry terminal and parked up. I walked over to the ferry office, that was closed. And saw that the ferry didn't sail until 18.30 that meant another day parked up. So cooker out and meal on, then bed. At seven the next morning I was awakened by all this noise, and looking out I saw that the ferry was coming in. As I looked at it, there was something very odd about it. Then I realised, it was an old P&O ferry from Dover. And you could still see the old paint work and P&O flag on the funnel. This was a wreck waiting to sink and I had to get on this thing and go 100 miles to Famagusta. That was eight hours sailing. I hope that the one from Limasol to Greece was better, that's 24 hours.

The mosque at Homs. The second most important city in Syria after Damascus.

Built for an old ruler, Khalid Al Walid

They call it the Triumphal arch. Part of the old city of Latakia and built by the Romans. The main seaport of Syria. And it was here that they discovered the oldest alphabet in the world, older than the Greek or Egyptian.

It was mid afternoon when the ferry office opened, by then I had done the tourist bit, but had walked round, and got pestered by the local kids and traders in the markets. Come back to the truck and made a meal and a brew, then done customs. I booked onto the ferry and was put on board. That's when I found out as 6.30 came and went and we are still in the port, that I was the only person on board and we would not sail until there were more passengers and cargo. We eventually sail at four on the Sunday morning. There are now three trucks and two cars on board and about fifty people. This thing has got engine trouble, and limps into Famagusta twelve hours later. I was never so glad to get off a ferry as I was this one.

Cyprus. It hadn't changed since I was out here with the UN forces in 1967. It was still a shit hole with everyone in uniform on the take. Both lots Turk and Greek, all the way up to the big prat Macarios. They were all corrupt. I had to pay the Greek Cypriot customs to stamp my TIR carnet, cash not cigs these prats were in for a shock soon. As the Turks would invade again and the island split in two with Famagusta going to the Turks.

I could have gone the coast road to Limasol, as it was shorter but not as safe as staying on the main highway. This meant that I had to go to Nicosia, then back down to the coast and then along to Limasol. This way you had less chance of being stopped and turned over by the civil police, as there was more traffic and the island was still under the UN. Patrolled and under watch towers. I pulled off the road just outside Limasol and made a brew. As I walked round the truck drinking my coffee a blue and white pulled in alongside me. The UN police. These lads are all Australian, and to make sure you knew where they came from they had a Kangaroo painted on under the police sign. It wasn't that often that they saw a Brit truck on the Island, apart from the military ones, and these lads would always spend a bit of time with us chatting and conning a brew. As they walked over to me I turned to them and said "blimy another two escapees". We sat and had coffee and a chat, mainly about my load and where I had picked it up, where I was going. Typical cops dead nosey. There was a couple of good points to come out of this meeting. The first was that there was a new ferry line now in Limasol, Minoan. Sailing to Patra in Greece. And two they would escort me into the dock and help with customs. That meant while they were with me I was not going to get fleeced by them, customs that is.

Into the town, along the front and into the dock. We pull up by the customs, and I have never seen customs that keen to do my papers and send me on my way to the ferry office. I thank the cops and pull down to the berth. A young lad shows me where to park and where the office is to book in, but the ferry will not be in until the morning. So I go and book in and take a walk round the dock, and find a small bar where I have a sandwich and a beer and watch as a Danish truck pulls in outside the customs. Half an hour later he comes out, not very happy. Looks as if they have made him pay, I call out to him and point over to my truck, he put his hand up and drives down to the berth. Half an hour later he is sitting down with me having a beer. He is not happy at all, having been given the run around by the Danish UN troops that he has delivered to. Instead of one delivery, they had him deliver to all five of their outposts, and then having to pay again for an empty trailer. No he was not happy, he wanted a few beers and a meal. Like an idiot I suggested we go to Hero square for the night.

This was not the right place to bring a Dane that wanted booze. Hero square just off the front where the War memorial stands in the middle of a square. All four sides of the square are bars and clip joints. Now he thinks he is in heaven. I find one bar that's not got many people in and go in for a meal. No meal for the Dane, one beer here and he says that he is going to have a look round a few of the clubs. So I tell him that I am staying here for the night, and will wait for him. But to leave his passport and wallet with me, and only take some of his money. Three hours later there's a UN police raid on a couple of the bars, and a few people are getting taken away in a police van and there he is swinging away at one of the Australian cops. Looks like I am going to have to bail him out as I have his passport.

The UN police have a very smart place on the sea front, and as I walk in there's the two cops that were at the dock with me. They take me to the duty officer, and I explain to him that he has a Danish civilian in his cells and I have his Passport and money, and how much is it going to cost to bail him out. As he has to be on the ferry tomorrow with his truck. They tell me not to worry, and they will bring him down to the dock in the morning when he has sobered up and slept it off and to hang on to his passport and money.

Sitting in the sun with a coffee and bacon and eggs on the go, the blue and white turns up with the Dane looking a bit under the weather. Takes one look at my breakfast and runs for the edge of the dock. A coffee and he will feel fine. Half an hour later I have a couple of Brit families parked next to me. Pity I have just put the frying pan away, but they can still smell the bacon sandwich next to my coffee. So I tell them that they can get fresh bacon at the little bar come shop.

The ferry comes in and berths. Two hours later we are getting ready to board, and I take a walk over to the ramp and look at the angel it is at as I only have six inch ground clearance on the trailer, and nine inch if I raise the air suspension on the axels. They load the two Brit campers then they load six trailers down each side then they call me over to load. Line up with the middle of the ramp and slowly reverse up and into the ferry. I soon have the crew there chaining truck and trailer down. With a change of clothes and my wash gear it's up to reception and book on. Get a cabin and shower first. All clean it's down to the bar for a coffee, and a chat with the crew. First thing I find out is that it will take 38 hours as it calls in at Rhodes and Crete on its way to Piraeus, great and I was told that it went to Patra. Looks like I have to drive through Athens when we get there.

38 hours on the ferry was not that bad. It was clean, and the food was good and cheap as was the beer and duty free. There were a few more cars and a coach came on before we sailed, but no other trucks. I spent most of my time out on the deck chatting to a few of the Brit tourists,

and making a couple of ship to shore phone calls one to Mavertons and one home to Joan, telling her that I was at last on my way home, and I was having more than a bloody week off. And with luck I should be home in a week. To date I had covered 10,875 Km driving, that's 6,797 Miles and used 3,750 Lt or 850 Gal of diesel. That was me doing the paper work and catching up with it all the expenses and costs, and just what money I had left against what I should have. And at the moment it was working out in my favour, as I had more than what I should have. Then I went through all my paperwork for the load that I had brought out, then the papers for the second load. That's when I started to realise that there was something missing from it. Three times I went through it. Then there it was. There was no Convoy Exceptional permit anywhere. How had that lad got it to where I took it off him. And why hadn't I checked as well. I had taken it for granted that there was one. Another ship to shore call to Mavertons and get Bert to DHL one out to Athens today, as I would be stuck in Piraeus till it arrived. When I got through to Bert and said that I would have a problem, all he said was no. Go to Harrys, there's an envelope waiting for you. The idiot brought it back.

Harrys truck stop. Just outside the dock at Piraeus. Soon as I was off of that ferry it was, park the truck and get over to Harrys and get the envelope with the permit. Then go back and do the customs. That out of the way, now I could relax and have a beer and find out when I could get a ferry over to Italy. I can get one the next day but I must go to Patra and book it, I can't do it from here. That's a five or six hour drive round to there through the

city of Athens and over the Corinth Canal. Sod it I will
not make it to their offices in Patra before they close
today. Means that I will have to go up tonight, to be there
for when they open first thing in the morning. A coffee
and a meal. And it's time to make a move. Out of the
dock and away through Athens. This is the first time that I
have driven through here at night, and it's strange how
things seem to be different in the dark. I got lost and
ended up outside one of the big hospitals. Ending up
being shown the way out of the city by an ambulance.

Corinth Canal. 4 miles long and dug out by hand.

Once out of the city it's a slow uphill drag along the
coast road to Elefsina, and Korinthos or Corinth, and the
canal. This bit I never did like. There are two Bailey

Bridges side by side over this deep cut. These things had been here since the second world war. The road way was timbers and they used to creak and groan as you went over them, and you could feel them move. That is a long way down to the water. Its motorway now though, but the bridges are still there for local traffic. Across the bridge and into the truck stop for a break, before the last part along the coast to Patra. An hour later and it's time to roll. I am just pulling out onto the road, and it starts to rain. As a driver in Greece this is the last thing that you need, as the roads now become doubly dangerous. First you have the normal danger, the nutty Greek car driver. And now you have the road surface. The tarmac has marble chippings in it, and in the wet the road is as slippery as ice. Well three hours later I pull into Patra and make my way down to the dock gates. Great they let me in and I park where they want me, so as to keep the gate and roadway clear. Normally if you don't have a booking for a ferry they keep you outside, but being a wide load they have let me in. Its coffee and bed.

Patra dock is full as I look out from my bunk. I was that knackered that after stripping off to my Y fronts I forgot to pull the curtains round. And there are a couple of groups of women and girls all looking in at me, with big grins and smiles on their faces. No good covering up now they have seen it all, so I sit up and put the kettle on, and ask if they want to come in for a coffee. There are no takers to my offer, so I get dressed, have my coffee and go over to the Minoan Line ferry office to book the next ferry. When I come out I am not a happy bunny. The ferry today is full, and there are no ferries for the next two days.

But the girl can book me on the ferry to Trieste tomorrow, or in three days to Ancona. Trieste it is then and another 30 hour sail, just today to get through as apart from eating and drinking there is not a lot to do in this Town.

By nine the following morning everyone is on board the ferry to Trieste, and its leaving the berth. One good thing at least this ferry will not be going into Igoumenitsa or any where ells on the way up. It's going to be about three in the afternoon when we dock, and four by the time I get off the ferry, and with only four trucks on it should be no problem with the Italian customs.

I stayed up most of that night so that I would sleep and be ready to go as soon as I got through customs. I changed a bit more money into Italian Lire, as I was not sure what it would cost to get through the Mt Blanc tunnel. I would get the French Francs in France.

Midday and I am awake. Shower and clean clothes, and into the bar for a coffee. Just finished the first cup when there is a call for all truck drivers to go down to their trucks. The ferry is pulling up to the berth at Trieste an hour and a half ahead of time. That means that I will at least make Venice in daylight, but I will also get the Rush hour there as well. I am called forward to drive off the ferry. Easier said than done. Air suspension pumped all the way up and I am still grounding. Now I have the Italian customs, police, and Dockers telling what to do to get it off the ferry. One of the customs officers comes over and takes my papers and 20,000 lire while I try to get off. In the end I call one of the deck officers and get him to call the other trucks up as far as the ramp, then get two trucks to drive up to the ship, their weight should be enough to hold the ferry down for me to drive off. Easy forward and I am off with a cheer from every one. The customs officer waves me over and gives me my papers back, less the 20,000 Lire. That was for using a Mickey mouse permit and no escort car. I am out of that dock gate and heading for the motorway. The rush hour at Venice is not that bad and I am soon round and on my way to Padova, and stop for a break at Verona services. As I walk back to the truck there are a couple of Caribineaire looking at the helicopter along with a coach load of tourists. That's all I need. As I walk over a police car pulls up alongside the trailer and the two cops join the rest in looking it over. In the cab and start up, turn all the flashing lights on, then get out and take a walk round checking that no one has messed about with the chains and straps and that everything is working, and say hi to the cops and Caribineaire. They want to know where I have brought it from and where it is going. One of the cops then tells me that I cannot drive tomorrow as it is holiday week end and as I am also a convoy exceptional I must be parked up by ten tonight.

No more hanging about, I am away out of there. It's going to be nonstop now to the other side of Milan. I think that I am breaking every law there is as I hit 100Km p h down the motorway past Brescia and ease up as I pass Bergamo airport, for the long left hand curve. If you're not expecting it, it will make you drift out and off the motorway. From there it's a strait run to Milan Est. Toll booths then across the top of the city. Monza, Via

Certosa, and up to the toll looking out for the police, as it is nearly ten as I pull up to take a ticket and drive on. Only get to the 1 Km marker for Novara services when there's an almighty bang and a bright flash of light up ahead. Then more explosions and fires. We come to a stop about 500 yards from what used to be the services. The restaurant that used to span the motorway has collapsed and both fuel forecourts have gone up as well.

By six the next morning the motorway has one lane clear in each direction, and everyone starts to walk back to their vehicles. All covered in dust and dirt and blood from digging people out of the rubble, no one is speaking, just the police and rescue teams thank us as we drive past and on our way. I pull off at Carisio, Italy's number one truck stop. Eight of us pulled in and parked that morning, and there were a lot of rumours going round as to what had happened and who had done it and why. And they all involved the mafia.

I spent the week end doing my final service to the truck and giving it a good wash and clean out. Along with sorting out my clothes, as a lot of them were beyond their best and fit for the bin. The rest went into the laundry. Then a call home to Joan and the boys. The Sunday was spent sleeping as everyone was waiting for ten o clock that night to pull out, mind some did risk it by leaving between nine and ten. But I would wait until five or six in the morning then head on up to Aosta for customs and that climb up to the tunnel. For if I was going to get any problems it was going to be at the top with the French.

The first thing was that I would need an escort car through and down the mountain.

Awake at five, and everything still closed I put the kettle on for a coffee. While that is boiling I go over to the spring and have a splash of freezing cold water to waken and freshen up. Coffee and it's time to go. First stop Aosta and the Italian customs. I have a break here at the same time and do a bit of shopping in the super market on the way out, and fill up with fuel at the Shell garage before Courmayeur and the last climb to the tunnel, and the customs. Yes I need an escort, and no I am not paying that as I don't wish to buy the bloody thing. In the end we agree a price and I go and wait, and wait. It's when the escort and tunnel control see me put all my lights on and start pulling forward, that they realise that I have had enough of their little game and close the tunnel from the French side so that I can pass through with the escort. The last bit of the mountain going down from the top to Sallanches he earns his money as the road twists and turns, and he gets the oncoming traffic to keep well in and stop before the bends to let me down. As this is two way and not the new motorway that's there now.

We pull in at Cluses as this is as far as he goes, and I am going to take a break. On the other side of the river they are building the new customs and putting the finishing touches to the end of the new motorway. It's time for a meal and a few hours sleep, before pushing onto the bake house for breakfast, as it is a good five or six hours from here, and I want to get it done over night and up to Paris by tomorrow night. Again from here the rule book is out of the window. And it's called, let's get home. Two in the morning and I am up and the kettle is on for coffee. Down to the river and splash cold water over my face, that's me wide awake now and ready to go.

There's no traffic about and I am making good time, and taking it slow and easy through the small towns and villages so as not to make a lot of noise and wake the local law up. I have a break just outside the village of Cerdon up by the grotto's. Just sitting there having a coffee when a CRS National police car pulls in and asks if I am ok and if I have any spare coffee, after chatting for about half an hour we both pull out and head for Pont Dain, Bourg en Bresse. From there I carry on up to the bake house, and find a space where I can pull right in off the road. Over breakfast I decide that from here I am going to use the motorway as far as Auxerre nord, then go back on the nationals to and round Paris on the Ho Chi Min trail. Only I can't take this load through Macon to get onto the motorway, and have to go back towards Bourge, then take a left to Cuisery and get the motorway at Tours.

Using all the road and their fore court I swing the rig round in a U turn and head off. Having to go this way it's going to take me a good five and a half hours to reach Auxerre so I will have a break at Avalon services or the one at the top of Bessie. That's the big hill towards Paris after Beaune. Into Cuisery and round the left hand bend over the river and up the hill into the village, when this Kermit sees me coming and all my lights on decides that he is still going to pull out and come past me the other way. No chance, he has to back up and let me through.

Just at the sharp right bend and a Dutch truck stops to let me round. This is why I should have an escort car with me. Half an hour later and I am at Tournus and getting onto the motorway. On past Beaune services and up to the top of Bessie, all full so it's on to Avalon. These are only small and I just manage to get parked. After an hour I am on my way again, and come off at Auxerre nord. Back on the national road and past the Algerians, another truck stop. Through Joigny and stop outside Sens for a coffee. I stop again at Fontainebleau for a break and change tacho cards, I stop here for a couple of hours then head off for Melun and the start of the Ho Chi Min trail via Meaux to Senlis and back onto the motorway north. By the time I reach Roye I am in need of a couple of hours sleep, so I pull into a parking area and put my old alarm on for two hours. Keep this up and I should be in Zeebrugge in the early hours of the morning, and on the midday sailing for Felixstowe and home.

Two hours later and I am up again and on the way up to Lille and the Belgium border to Kortrijk. Both customs done and now for a coffee. Don't let the Belgians think that I am in a hurry. From here it's not that far to Gent and then into the Total garage outside Zeebrugge ferry terminal. Fill right up with fuel and get a few cartons of cheap cigs, then it's into the dock and park.

Wash kit and a clean change of clothes, it's over to the freight drivers lounge for a shower, and shave. Change of clothes and relax with a couple of beers and a couple of cheese and ham rolls while I sit here and wait for the ferry staff to arrive so that I can get booked on for home.

Turn Round.

7am and the Townsend ferry girls opened up the check in desks. As the shutters went up, I just stood there looking at this notice on the wall behind them. In big red letters it had, Maverton Drivers. DO NOT SHIP, PHONE IN. Ship trailer back unaccompanied only. The girl must have seen my face as she called me over and gave me the phone. It was already ringing. Johnny Spiller was on the other end, as all I said was "John its smurf". Then out came all the apologies and how long I had been out already, and that they had spoken to Joan about it, and that we would be paid full trip for each trailer that we did that had been dumped. That's when I cut him off by saying "how many trailers we F***ING talking about". "15 between the five of you, only three each smurf". Half an hour we were on the phone for, and when I hung up the girl asked for my name and truck number, then gave me a really large brown envelope. Inside were the papers and details of three low loaders. The first was just outside Zeebrugge at the Shell garage. This one was the important one and must be done. Only take the papers for this trailer. Leave the rest with Townsend.

Well one look at the paperwork told me why this had to go first, its loaded with two 432 APCs, armoured personnel carriers. And it is routed the same way that I have just come back, only the destination is Aden, Yemen. The only good thing is I am not one of the two that are going to Esfahan in Iran, who ever cops that has some real bad roads to travel. Still let's get rid of this trailer down by the berth and the papers into the office then go and find this trailer at the Shell garage.

It's been dropped in front of the exit gate but not blocking it, so I get under it, couple up and push it to the back of the parking area. After checking it over and finding that nothing has been touched or taken, and the chains are all still tight and all marker and flashing lights work. And who ever dumped it was in a hurry as he has left his number plate on the trailer. Into the garage to make another call. I have to collect the running money from Schenker at the border between Kortrijk and Lille where I will also have an escort car to take me all the way to Ancona in Italy, the escort is coming out from England on Sunday and will be at the border first thing Monday. And its only Friday morning now.

To hell with it I spend an hour on the phone talking to Joan and the boys. Mavertons can pay for it, and I can tell that she is not well pleased that I am not on my way home, like I had said I was. But going back out again. The money was OK that was there every four weeks and I had a pay rise, I was now or she was getting £1400. After stoppages that was £350 a week clear plus what I was making out on the trip, all told about £500 now that was good money in the 70s and 80s.

Sitting at the back of the garage having a couple of beers and going through the expenses of the last trip and the money I had left I owed them £10. And I had £235. In my hand, that went directly into my wallet. The total mileage for the trip back to here was 12407 Km and 7749 Miles 4360 Lt diesel and 969 Gallons. And I now had to do it all over again. I had been away nine weeks, ten on Monday. That escort car was going to have to wait for me. I had to go into Brussels and get four visas done before I went anywhere. To get the four done in the same day I would be very lucky, that was Syria, Jordan, Saudi and Yemen, they were going to cost about £150. Mind they are open on Saturdays. I will give them a try in the morning.

I spent all day Saturday going from one embassy to another getting transit visas. Syria, Jordan and Saudi gave me multiple entry visas. The Yemen visa was the hardest to get, they wanted a letter from someone in Yemen to vouch for me. I told them to contact their defence minister, and ask him where he wanted these APCs as I would leave them on the border with Saudi. After an hour he put the visa in my passport. I had started at the Syrian embassy at nine that morning and it was five in the evening as I walked out of the Yemen embassy, to get a cab back to the truck at the motorway services just outside Brussels and the first cup of coffee that day.

Sunday midday and I am off to the border at Kortrijk and park up. The French customs will not open until 10pm, but the Belgian customs are there so I go over and get that half done, then drive over to the French half. Schenker is not going to be open until either ten tonight or nine in the morning, and that's when the escort car should arrive. So I settle down for the night and get some sleep.

Only to be wakened at 10.30pm by a girl from Schenker. She has my money and wants me to come over to the office and get it now, as they don't like having that amount of cash there. She takes a photocopy of my passport and hands me the cash in an envelope, asking me to check it and then sign for it. £2,000. All in sterling, and with that in my wallet its back to the truck and sleep. The escort driver can wake me when he gets here. But first I think I will get the French customs done. That's one less to do in the morning.

6.30am and I have had a coffee and we are on our way into Lille, with the escort following behind. Only on the national roads would he be in front. He had done this trip a couple of times before and was forever on the CB telling me to slow down, as I was only allowed to do 40 MPH. I got that pissed off, I told him if he didn't like it he could turn round now and head for Calais and piss off home. And he could also forget the rule book, as we would be in Ancona Friday morning, shit or bust, as I had a ferry to catch. And I would tell him where and when we would stop for breaks and sleep.

I kept him going till we hit the Ho Chi Min trail and told him to pull in at a truck stop at Meaux for an hour's break. From there with him in front now I pushed him. Through Fontainebleau and on to Joigny, he must have thought that we were stopping at the Algerians, as he pulled into the truck park. I kept going and he soon came out of there in a hurry and got back in front. We went back onto the motorway and pulled in at Auxeaire services. I told him that we would get our heads down here for a few hours, and go through the night to the Blanc. He was not impressed with that idea at all, and kept on about the rules. I lost it with him, and told him that he had two choices. Either he kept up with me or he f***ed off now back to Calais as I didn't give a shit what he did or said. With that he went and phoned his boss while I had a coffee. He was at the phone waving to me to come over to him, his boss wanted a word with me. Now this prat pissed me off. He started to lay the law down, saying that his driver was in charge and that I would do what he said and run by the book or he would phone my boss. That was it I lost it. I told him to go ahead and phone them, I even gave their home phone numbers to him, and told him what his driver could do, as out here I was god and put the phone down on him.

Midnight and I have the kettle on for a coffee, before pulling out. I look in the escort van and he is not in there, he has gone and booked himself into the motel. And he has parked the van about a foot away from my front bumper, thinking that was going to keep me here till he was ready. I put a notice on his wind screen. You were told. And used the tuck to push the van out of the way.

He must have driven like a lunatic to catch me. I was parked up and had made a meal and was just clearing up when he pulled in behind me. He came at me saying that he was in charge of the route and how I had to do it his way by the book, or he would report me to the ministry in England, all the time pocking me in the chest. I took so much of it then it was my turn to pock. Right on the end of his nose then pushed him into the river telling him to go back home to mummy, as he was not ready to play with the big boys yet. And it was time I got a bit of sleep.

The escort was nowhere to be seen when I woke up and made a brew. A check of all the lights and chains, and I was ready for the climb up the Blanc to the tunnel. No traffic all the way to the customs hut at the split for the tunnel. At the top I was called forward and not onto the parking, as the tunnel escort was waiting to go back through. That saved a bit of time.

Mt Blanc tunnel French entrance above and Italian below

Out the Italian side and park. Upstairs in the main building and change a bit of money, and a coffee in the bar. Back to the truck and pull forward to the Italian customs, show my TIR carnet and carry on down the mountain to the Shell garage and fill up then on to Aosta and the main customs. An hour and a half later I am pulling in and parking up near to the transit office. All paperwork signed and stamped and 10,000 Lire for Mickey permit. Out the gate and on to Carisio for the night and find out about a ferry booking.

There's not many here as I pull in and park up. But over the back I spy the escort van parked up next to a Carmans transport, (now Brit European) and if he is in the bar he will have seen me come in and park. Let's see what he has been talking about. He is at the far end of the bar with a few other drivers, I totally ignore him as Mario the barman hands me a beer without asking what I want and shakes my hand, I notice that he is pointing at me and nodding his head in my direction as he talks to the others. I decide that I am going to wind this little shit up. "Oy shit for brains" I call out to him, "you and me aint finished yet, your with me all the way to Aden". That part was true. He was, the next bit was the wind up. "your arss is mine pal for the next three weeks, so listen and learn cos you're on your own on the way back." He went pale and quiet. "phone your boss, your mine pal." As I stand there with a big smile on my face looking at him. He heads for the phone, and the other drivers come and ask if it was true that he was going with me. I told them to wait and see.

He comes out of the phone, asks for a beer and his lips are trembling as he is near to tears. He had told Carman that he would quit, and was told that if he did he could make his own way home, leaving the van there and he would not be paid. Plus his name would go in the transport drivers black list, and he would never work in transport again. Knowing Carman he would.

I took the lad outside and had a word with him and told him, that on the Middle East you had your own rules. And if he listened and learnt he would be OK. To do what I told him when I told him he would make it. Now all we had to do was get his visas sorted out in Athens. And that I would phone Carman and tell him to get £1,000. Out to Western union in Patra to cover visas, fuel and the odd back hander along the way. He had sent this lad out unprepared for the job, and I would screw everything I could out of him for the lad. As far as the lad and I knew he was only going to Ancona. It wasn't until I had made a call to Mavertons from Aosta and was told the plan had changed. No one had thought about telling the lad.

I got a fax from Minoan Line in Ancona about the ferry bookings. The earliest that they could get was for the following Monday from Venice, or the Tuesday from Ancona, for both me and the escort. I got the lads passport and faxed back our details and the reg numbers of both vehicles for the Tuesday sailing from Ancona. That meant that we now had three days here to kill, four if you included today. Then run down to Ancona on the Monday and park up in the dock. That was the trouble with all the ferries, from June to September they took all the tourists first, and the rest of the year they used to fight each other to get the freight. Half an hour later I had the faxback with our confirmed bookings.

At Carisio there's not a lot that you can do really, there's a trout lake that you can go and do a bit of fishing out towards Vercelli, or the swimming pool at Biella. So apart from eat, drink, and sleep that was about it. Or you could always wash your truck down. The week end was mayhem there was over a hundred trucks there. And the normal drunken fights. All Europe V Germany, then half an hour later everyone was back in the bar, and best of mates again.

Sunday night and nearly everyone was pulling out. I told the lad that we would leave early, so that we could get round Milan and onto the Bologna motorway before the traffic built up. So after a meal and a coffee we turned in. At five the next morning I woke him with a cup of coffee. Half an hour later we were pulling out on our way to Milan. Going past Novara services I noticed that the garage and pumps were up and working and that they had demolished the old bridge restaurant and were putting a new one across.

With hardly any traffic we were soon round Milan and heading south. If we could keep this sort of speed we should be there on the dock by tea time, just so long as Bologna was clear of any hold ups. Past Modena services and off at the Bologna Ancona split. We pull in the other side of the city for a beak. It's not long till we are past Rimini and following the Adriatic coast down to Ancona. Down the hill past the hospital and turn right at the main coast road and into Ancona. Round past the fish dock and along the wall to the customs at the port entrance. It's a good job it's not that busy and there are only a few trucks behind us as I finish customs and move into the dock and park over at the Minoan berth, a quick wash and over to the bar for a meal and a few beers.

Ancona dock ferry terminals taken from the cathedral walls.

Woken the next morning by the ferries coming in and all the traffic and tourists walking about. We both go over to the office and book in. The deck officer is there and he tells us that as soon as everything is off the ferry he wants us to back on while the tide is low, and the ramp is level with the berth. I back on and he puts me in the centre and up to the ramp, and sends the escort up on the top deck where he will send the tourists and fridge trucks. Open deck.

Twenty hours on here to Patra via Igoumenitsa. And two days wait for the ferry to Cyprus from Piraeus. It was no contest when we got off at Patra. The sun was hot and the sea was warm. Up to the Shell garage, park up and walk back a hundred yards to the beach for the rest of the day, and tonight we would park at Korinthos by the canal. It was six that evening as we pulled in at the Corinth truck stop, parked and walked up to the bridges over the canal. We were in luck as there was a cruise ship passing through, and you look down at the passengers who are waving up at us.

A steady drive down and through Athens and round to the dock at Piraeus, only to be turned away by the customs as they tell us that there is no ferry to Cyprus. It sunk on its way here. They let us park just outside the gate, and we walk over to Harrys so that I can sort out another booking. Failing that it will mean going all the way up to Volos and getting the ferry direct to Tartus in Syria, now that is a ship waiting to sink.

I have a bigger problem though, and one that has to be sorted out now. The lad hasn't got any visas. Shit that means we are going to be here at least another two days sorting them out, then another couple of days getting up to Volos. That's going to be another week gone without getting anywhere, and I am starting to get a bit pissed off to say the least. Two days later I have the booking from Volos for the two of us, and he now has all his visas, and we can at last start moving. I wait till late that night before moving out, as Athens is a hell hole to drive through at the best of times. Harry has given the lad directions how to get to the Lamia road, and from there it's strait on to Volos. The thing was, if you got directions from Harry about Athens you got every cross road and traffic light. You just could not get lost. The lad out in front we were away, and as we started to leave Athens he pulled in and parked outside a garage. He thought that we were stopping here for the night, well I soon put him strait on that score. We were booked on the ferry the next day, and we were going there overnight. We could have a brew here and again at Velestino where we turned off for Volos. Through Thiva and Lamia, and as we came up to the turn off at Velestino I flashed my lights and pulled over outside the Coca Cola factory. We would have a quick break here as the road down to Volos was not the best and it would soon get busy with fridge trucks, as there was a large fish market and fish port there. An hour and a half later we were stopping outside the customs office, and as soon as we came out of there we were getting called to the berth and told to back on board. We were the only truck going, all the others were just trailers and cargo.

Good thing it was still dark when we got on, as I think if the lad had seen the state of this tub he would not have got on. Held together by rust, the drivers cabin was a twenty foot container welded to the deck with bunk beds. As for the food, well not even the gulls would eat it, the only thing that was edible was the bread and you had to look that over first. For four days on there we lived on bread and our own food from the truck, and I was a happy boy when I spotted the lights of Tartus getting nearer.

As I drove off and parked over by the custom, I noticed that there were no other trucks parked. That could mean that we would be allowed to leave there and then, or we would have to wait for a convoy from Latakia to the Jordanian Border at Ramtha. It all depended on who was in charge and how many cigs he was given, as they were not that keen on you going unescorted past Damascus. Not bad only two packets and $10. And we are stamped up, letter to run unescorted to Ramtha. Not bad going.

Out of the docks and away towards Homs. The other side of Homs I get the lad to pull over off the road. While the kettle is on the go I draw a rough map of our route to Damascus using the desert road running parallel to the Lebanon border, through the villages of Khasiya, Al Burei where we will stop for a break. Then on to Nabk and Mnin just outside Damascus. The one thing that I impress on him is the fact that from here on in its desert road to Damascus, as we will not be taking the route the convoys take, and to stay on the track at all times. We stop for the night at Mnin a small village to the north of Damascus. We will get an early start and go round the city and stop at the Ghabagheb fuel point for a break and fill up.

We are round Damascus and pulling up at Ghabagheb fuel point at ten o clock, fill up and make a brew. Then it's on to Sheik Mishim, and Dera , where we learn that there is a hold up at the Ramtha border so we have another brew. Then on to the border. Where's the hold up, both sides are empty and in half an hour we are pulling into the Jordanian side. As we are the only ones there they have decided that they will take their sweet time getting us through, but I play along with them. Telling them that I am going to stop overnight in Amman and go sightseeing in the morning then I am going to go down the Dead sea coast road and the border road to Aqaba. That meant going all the way down the Wadi Al Jayb Then cross into Saudi Arabia at Haql on the Gulf of Aqaba. They said only mad English would want to go that route. Everyone went on the new highway to Ma-an and crossed the border at Qalat el Mudawara. Seeing that I was not bothered by them hanging about as we only had about 80 Km to do they let us go at 6pm, and two hours later I was pulling over outside a small motel with a truck park alongside it.

Stop over motel Amman from truck park.

View of Al Rashid square from roof of Al Rashid
Hotel, and our tour guides in national

dress

The gold
market

Royal Palace

That evening we had a meal along with one small beer. Then we were asked by a young girl if we would like to be escorted round the city to see some of the sights. Great. The next morning was the same only this time we had two guides. But it was mid afternoon when we took our leave of them and headed for Jerusalem only turning left before we got to the Israel border and headed south on the dead sea coast road and ran down as far as Mazra. The lad just had to go in for a dip and see if he would float. It was lucky for him that there was a bit of water still in the stream to wash the salt off him when he came out. After a good meal it was time to turn in, as tomorrow would be a long and hard drive down the Wadi Al Jayb to Aqaba our next overnight stop.

I don't know where the lad got the idea that the desert was rolling sand dunes. He was learning fast that it was the most unforgiving and harsh place to be. Dry and lifeless most of the time with the odd bit of scrub and the odd scorpion. Rock instead of sand, hard sharp climbs and mountains instead of rolling dunes, and I could see by his driving that he was respecting the country and road. He stopped at Shamar an oasis and stopping place of the Bedouin. One family were setting up their tents. This was done by the women. The men had stockade the animals and were having a drink of strong Arabic coffee. As soon as they found out that we were English, they called us to join them. The coffee is ok if it is sweet and washed down with cool lemon water. At first the lad didn't know what to do but after a while we were all chatting in broken English and sign and he ended up playing football with the kids and loved it.

The next morning when we got up, the Bedouin had packed and gone without making a noise. I was over at the well getting water and having a wash, before putting the kettle on. That's when I noticed the four Israeli soldiers walking towards the well with the lad. That's when I politely told the four of them to F/O to their own side of the border, and that I would report the incursion by them to the Jordanian army, and that they had cut the fence. They kept saying that they wanted water, when in fact they wanted to get up close to the APCs that I had on. So again I told them to fuck off and they could have all the water they wanted at the north end of the border fence, and they knew I meant the dead sea. And that there was no way that they were about to get near the well or my truck. They went back through the fence as I gave them the one finger salute. 5 Km down the road we met up with the Jordanian army and I reported what had happened.

That afternoon we are at the outskirts to Aqaba and there is the gulf in front of us. A cop pulls up next to us on his motor bike, looks us over and decides that we and the trucks are in need of a wash before he will let us into his nice clean city, and points us in the direction of the dock and the truck wash. This is Jordan's only sea port and it is busy 24/7 even Friday.

Truck and van washed I find a make shift shower where we can get cleaned up and put some clean clothes on to look human again, then it's off to find somewhere for a meal and a coffee. Leaving the truck and van near the dock security. Two hours later we return and get our heads down for the night, and knowing just what prats the

Saudi customs can be I intend to be there on the border
early as its only about half an hour away, but we could be
there all day. In Saudi Arabia a couple of things stand out.
The first is that there are two types of people, the rich and
the poor. And are they poor. The next is that the Saudi
men are bone idle and think that manual work is below
them. Nearly all the work here is done by migrant
workers, and foreign companies. My way to describe a
Saudi is. "plenty of money, but no brain." A Saudi will
pay for anything, even the letters after his name to make
you think he is educated.

The sun is just coming up as we pull into the customs.
As we are the only ones there the Jordanians clear us
through then go to morning prayer. Not the Saudi, he
waits till he sees us walking over to him then he walks off
along with the rest of them. This could take an hour, so
it's time to put the kettle on. And for me to start on the
Saudis. I had bought some bacon from a Christian butcher
in Aqaba, it's time for egg and bacon as well. That smell
gets everywhere, and they are going to get rid of us quick
when they come back. We are both standing at the desk
with our papers all laid out for them, coffee in one hand
and egg and bacon sandwich in the other. Two of them
stamped and signed our papers and got us out in ten
minutes.

From there it's over a mountain to the split for Al Bir
and Tabuk for an overnight stop. By now I am walking
about in full Arab dress, as it's a lot more comfortable
than Jeans and T shirt, and cooler. The next day we are on
our way to Tayma and Medina, where we turn right and

head back for the Red Sea and Rabigh. A couple of hours stop here then a push to Jeddah and the Brit compound of Lang Civil Engineering. This firm is building Jeddah container dock. But all I want is to use their shower and laundry while we stop overnight here with them. With luck we could be back here in five days.

A good night's sleep, shower and meal. And all our laundry done, breakfast and coffee, we bid the lads good bye till our return. We have a hard two days drive left in front of us to Aden and delivering this load.

With the Red Sea on our right we head south for Al Lith and Al Qunfudhan with the high Asir mountains on our left all the way to Jizan, about 10Km before the Yemen border our last overnight stop before Aden. And I wanted to be fresh and ready for the Yemen customs as these could be downright awkward and make problems where there aren't any. But I have the ace card if they do start being funny. I have a letter in Arabic and English to off load them and leave them with the chief Yemen customs officer.

That night we had fresh fish, the lad had a fishing rod in the van, don't know what type it was but it tasted ok. Next morning we drove into the customs, cleared the Saudi in an hour then drove over to the Yemen side. I asked one of the officers that spoke English what the time was. He told me it was seven and asked why. So I told him if I was not clear to go by nine I would follow his governments instructions and unload them here and showed him the letter. Ten minutes later we are on our way to Al Hudaydah, and Ta izz and our last set of mountains to go over before dropping down to Aden. At the top we pull in and stop for a brew and look down at Aden off in the distance and the blue of the Gulf of Aden beyond. At the bottom I pull in again, we have to find a Military base where these APCs are for. And the best way to find it is with the aid of a local cop. And with what we have on it will not be long before someone informs them that we are here having a brew. Fifteen minutes and we have six, two cars and four motor bikes. We have an all round escort for all of two Km. In the main gates and parked up by a parade square. Four Yemen army officers and a Brit officer followed by two Brit sergeants. None of this lot can get over the way I am dressed. All I want is for them to sign and stamp my papers so that I can then get these off my trailer and away back up the road.

There are two Yemen soldiers about to start undoing the chains, when I shout for them to stop. I will do it. With a long steel bar I go round and hit each chain dog and release the chains. If they hit you when they spring open, they can take your arm or head off. They are pulled down tight with four foot steel pipes. The lad then helps lower the ramps, and I tell them that I will take them off the trailer, after that they can play with them. With them off I tell the lad to put the van on the trailer over the axels and strap it down. With the ramps up we are ready to go, but first we are offered the showers and a meal then we are on our way back to the mountain and over to Ta izz for the night. It's gone midnight as I pull off the road and park about half way down the mountain towards Ta izz, I am shattered and all I want is a coffee and a bit of kip.

The next morning sees us into Saudi and up to Jizan for our first break and a quick dip in the red sea, then it's on to Jeddah along the side of the Asir mountains with a quick stop at Al Lith and into the Lang compound outside Jeddah docks. Again it was shower, laundry, meal, and the use of their phone to call home and Mavertons. And that when I got the good news. I had to recover two of our trucks on the way home, one in Iraq and one in Syria. I had to wait there for the full directions as to where the truck was in Iraq, and the second may be a bit of a problem, as driver had taken wrong track and was now in no man's land between Syria and Lebanon, just west of Homs at Tall Kalakh. And Carmans lad had to fly back from Riyadh to London.

I got called into the Lang transport office as the fax had arrived. They had a big map of Saudi and Iraq on the wall, and I started looking for where this truck was and how to get there. The quickest way was from here, back up to Al Qalib and across the north Nafud desert to Al Jawf to Badana on the pipe line at A5 then the desert trail across the border at Judalda Arar, and with luck 120 Km out into the Iraqi desert was the village of Nokhaib. But first I had to get the lad to the airport at Riyadh, at least his ticket home was there with Saudi Air. And he had more luck, there was a car from Lands going there overnight. That meant I could get on my way in the morning. That was when I realised that I still had the bloody van on the trailer. I had all the paperwork for it and the keys, I put a for sale notice on it asking for offers in US Dollars only. By 7.30 the next day I was $550 richer, and empty trailer.

Recovery.

With the Dollars in my wallet and a last cup of coffee I was on my way again to Al Qalib and the trip across the desert. I made the oasis at Al Hawja that day. Its 500 Km from here to the border, and another 100 to where the truck is. That's a good two days hard drive of desert, and there's the Saudi and Iraqi customs at Arar. The next day I only made it to about fifty Km shot of Badana crossing, when the sky started turning red. A sand storm was blowing in from the west, and I started looking quickly for somewhere that I could get the truck down into a wadi or deep dip and turn the cab away from the wind. Four hours later and it has past, so I drive back up onto the track. That takes me half an hour, and I can only just make out where the track is. It's too dark to go on so I make a brew and settle down for the night.

I am away at first light and nonstop to Arar border. There's one of Astrans trucks there on his way to Jeddah. We have a brew and a chat, and he tells me that he has seen the truck, and that it is in a large gully still on its wheels and with the trailer. That's empty, but there was no sign of the driver. It was about two or three Km this side of Nokhaib. We were on our second coffee when the Saudis called us over. Our papers were done, what papers, all I had was my passport and empty papers. We shock hand and parted. The Iraqis knew all about the truck and that it was me that was picking it up. The driver had left the keys with them three days ago having got a lift to Amman Jordan and flying home. Bastard, fucking little bastard. Now I was left with recovering it on my own, and if it's like Astrans driver said, I had my work cut out.

I nearly missed it in the fading light. It was down in a gully alright, looked as if he had driven it in and parked it. Too late and dark to get it out now, have to do it at first light while it was cool. In the morning I go and check that it will start, then it's a question of do I try and back the lot out the same way it came in or leave the trailer where it is and pull the unit out on my trailer winch. Then again there is only me, and that no good bastard has left me in the shit. I decide that it's going to come out the way it went in. A cup of coffee, and I start it up, into reverse brakes off and give it everything it's got My foot was flat to the floor and it just took off up the slope and right across the track. Five seconds later and I would have taken out a Hungarian truck, good job he had figured out what I was doing as I hadn't seen him. He turned out to be a good lad, gave me a hand dropping the trailer and putting the truck up on my trailer and chaining it down, after we had let most of the air out of the tyres. I put the kettle on and made a brew for both of us and gave him $20 for stopping, but he would not take it. That's what the job was all about. You helped each other out, as you never knew when you may need help. All you wanted at the end was a brew, not payment. You were all truckers doing the same job. Mind I did tell him to help himself to a couple of the wheels and tyres off of the trailer. As I was going to take them off anyway, or the Arabs would have them tonight. Two hours later and the trailer has all three axels on heaps of rock, I have four super singles and the Hungarian has the other two as well as the spare. Another coffee and we both go our own ways, me towards Rutbah and him to Kerbala.

It's getting dark as I come off the desert and onto the Rutbah highway. I push on and reach the edge of town before pulling over and parking up. I make a quick meal and a brew then turn in for the night. By midday the next day I am through the border and into Syria. It's a day's drive to Homs from here, so it's going to be tomorrow afternoon before I get to where the other truck is. Come off the Damascus road at Sab Biyar and take the desert road across for Homs. I keep going well after dark as far as Furqlus, about 15 Km from Homs. Its pitch black and gone midnight as I find somewhere to pull off and park. I am awakened by an old man knocking on my cab. I have parked on a road junction and am blocking the exit with the trailer, so I pull forward and make a brew before going on to find this other prat of ours. And this one had better be there.

There he is, it's the little jock. He comes out into the road and waves me down as I come to the village of Tall Kalakh, I pull in and park. He takes me over to a coffee shack where we sit and chat about his truck. He is on his way back from delivering to a place outside Beirut called Sayda, or Sidon. On his way up to the border he had been having gear box problems, and between the Lebanese and Syrian customs it had finally blown up leaving him stuck there in the middle. But he had now managed to get a tow out and through the customs, it had cost him $50 but at least he was through. He wanted to know what we were supposed to do with his trailer. Easy I said, strip the wheels off it or sell it. We striped it, then put the truck on the trailer after taking the other one off first, and using the winch to drag it on and up the front, then put the other one back on. Now it was time to get home, first stop Latakia and the ferry.

Seven days later we are getting of the ferry at Ancona. The only phone calls that we make are to our wife's. With two drivers this old truck will not be stopping very often till we reach Zeebrugge. We had one meal on the way and that was at the bake house in France. Apart from coffee breaks we kept going. 32 hours from Ancona to Zeebrugge. And the ferry to Felixstowe. The first phone call to Mavertons was from Romford. They knew we were on our way, and were waiting for us at the yard. I had been away just over 4 months on this trip. Lou Sains gave me £1000. Cash as a bonus, and in the next breath he told me to be back here in two weeks, ready to go again.

It was great being home, and I kept the boys of school for a week. I had to get nearly all new clothes as the others were falling apart in the wash. We went out every single day that first week with the boys, then Joan thought that I had better get on and do a few of the jobs that needed doing around the house. But the two weeks soon came to an end when on the Sunday morning Sains and Worth pulled up at the top of the road with the truck. No trailer just the unit.

The four of us sitting in the kitchen. Me, Joan, Sains, and Worth drinking coffee as they explained that there were 15 trailers all loaded for Iraq and Iran with generators. That had been dumped in Belgium and Holland by owner drivers. All we had to do was deliver the trailers and loads to their destinations. In other words pull the pin and leave the lot. Back for the next one solo, unit only. But we had to do the Iranian loads first as the weather would soon close in on the mountains in Iran. There would be six of us on the morning ferry from Felixstowe to Europort as all six loads for Tehran were at Breda truck stop on the Belgium border. All the papers were with Schenker along with the running money. We were to keep in contact first and last calls from the Telex at Ankara.

As they left Sains slipped Joan £500 saying I should have had three weeks off really. All my gear went back into the truck ready for the morning. With no customs to do at Felixstowe it meant that I could have a lay in, there was no need to be there till nine to book on.

This was going to be a fun trip. Six of Mavertons Mavericks together all the way to Tehran and back. We found all six trailers parked up together outside the Schenker office. This dump had been planned, as this was where they had to pick up the running money. The staff here were not amused at having to give out a second lot of money for the same trailers. We sorted out all the paper work for each trailer, signed for the money, and went off to do the Dutch and Belgian customs, and so started another trip, only this time we knew that we would be away more than one trip. An hour later we have all done both customs and are having Frickendel and chips for dinner before heading off. Only its taking time to decide where we are stopping tonight. Aachen, Frankfurt, or Wurzburg. When I say if we are going that far, why not go to Geiselwind. They all look at me as if I am mad. Ok there's a cop shop next to it but we are going to get the same fine if we get stopped at Frankfurt, plus we can have a beer there. That settled it Geiselwind it was.

It was not a very exiting run down to the Telex at Ankara, ok we cancelled a few days on the way. Like, one at the hotel Wien in Budapest. One at the National Belgrade, another at the Londra Kapikula, not including the 34 hours to clear Turk customs. And another at Istanbul. By the time we pulled in at the Telex we were only four days behind, and the weather was getting cold and wet. We had a few beers and a meal and turned in for the night. It was the next morning while we all having breakfast in the restaurant, little jock turned round and asked who had Iranian visas. Everyone went silent and we all looked at each other. No one had, great. That now meant that we each needed a letter from the customer in Iran, i.e the Iranian electricity ministry inviting us to Iran. Phone call, panic stations can't get England on the phone. Two taxis every one down to the Iranian Embassy with all our paperwork. Four hours later and each $50 lighter we have our visas and are back at the Telex, panic over. The rest of the day we spent servicing and checking out our trucks and trailers and topping up the ante freeze and getting our brake lines and air tanks free of water by putting ether down the air lines, then putting a couple of gallons of petrol into the diesel to stop that from turning to jelly. If it's wet and cold here, it's going to be white and freezing the closer we get to Iran and those bloody mountains, especially that Mt Kuh e Sahand. The whole of northern and western Iran is mountains all the way down the gulf, and from Tehran and Esfahan east is desert, and salt flats. Three days from Ankara and we are at the border, Dogubayazit / Bazargan, and there's snow on the ground.

Mt Ararat. Winters on the way.

This is all we needed to see. It was going to get worse yet. The one thing they haven't got is good snow ploughs to keep the mountain passes clear, you had to rely on the military to do that. We all get cleared and head off, making it as far as Khvoy, where we park up two abreast the front two turning round and go grill to grill with the two behind, and the last pair right up to the back of the trailers in front to keep the wind off of the radiators. We are past Tabriz and round Mt Kuh e Sahand to Mianeh for a break. We have to make Qazvin tonight so as to be able to make Tehran airport tomorrow at Eslamshahr. We have decided that we are not dumping the trailers, we are going to take them back into Turkey, and sell them.

A day and a half at the airport and we are clear and empty and on our way back to the border. There's more snow down and we are forced to put our snow chains on. Four days to the border, there's no one there and customs are surprised to see the six of us roll in. In two hours we are through both the Iranian and the Turk, into Dogubayazit and park. Having just got the kettles going the Turk cops tell us that we must move and not park here tonight as more snow is coming. Fuck it we have our brew and head off. By the time we get to Erzurum its dark and there's a cold wind blowing. Can't get into the truck parking area as it has been blocked off so we just stop for another brew and head off again. We are at Sivas before we find a place where we can all get parked up, no brew but into our bunks.

Nine hours later little jock is waking every one with a hot mug of coffee, and the news that Emmet at the Telex has found a transport firm in Ankara that will buy all six trailers from us, if we take them to his yard on the way to the Telex. But it must be in the morning after his trucks have gone. He will pay us in English pounds,£500 each cash. The yard is between Kirikkate and Ankara, and its eight o, clock as we each back in from the road and park them at the bottom of his yard and drop them. Giving him all the paperwork for them and putting the cash in our pockets. Then it was the Telex and a phone call to the yard and find out where we were going next, and a call home.

We stayed together all the way back to Austria and Germany where we split up to pick up the dumped trailers and head back south to Iraq and Baghdad. I did three trailers from Germany selling them on the way through Turkey, and one out of Austria that I reloaded from Schenker in Salzburg back to England, well Scotland in fact. That was where little jock and I met up again and ran back to the yard together.

Both our trucks and trailers were in shit order. We could have told the German BAG (ministry of transport inspectors) that when they pulled us both in at the inspection point at Munchen. They just could not believe the state of our trucks or how we had got that far with them. Having run out of spare wheels I had the centre axel chained right up with only the brake drums showing. Only four wheel arches and they were held on by odd nuts and bolts. No wheel arches on the rear drive axel of the truck, the snow chains had taken them off along with the rear lights and the front grill was held on with rope. And the front bumper had been welded back on top of a steel beam. And little jocks wasn't any better. Sods fined us a hundred D Mark and told us to disappear out of Germany. That night we hid up the back of Geiselwind truck stop, and set off again early in the morning and one hit it all the way to Aachen Heerlen the German Dutch border. And tucked ourselves out of the way at the back on the Dutch side of the parking area, while we went and done customs.

Everywhere we went we got bad looks from people, and they would stand back from us. Well we were a bit smelly and unshaved and our trucks looked as if they had got out of a scrap yard. But who gave a shit. Me and little jock were on double what these European drivers were on and we did more work than they did. We drove to Europort overnight and when we went in to do Dutch customs. They knew who we were and where we had been as soon as they saw our trucks, or what was left of them they took our papers and told us to go and get a shower. When we came out of the shower all our cloths had gone and two pairs of overalls were there in place. And outside we could see the Dockers had put the fire hoses onto our trucks. We asked if we could wash our clothes while we waited for the ferry.

Our clothes and trucks washed and us showered we were booked on the night crossing to Felixstowe. A few beers a good evening meal and beak fast in the morning along with our duty free we drove off at Felixstowe and were bonded forward to Aberdeen Scotland to clear customs there. Our agent there, Schenker gave us each an Envelope from Mavertons along with our bond notes and gate pass. Over to the drivers canteen for a coffee and look at our letter. Well it came as a bit of a shock. We were redundant as soon as we got back to the yard. The letter was short and to the point. It went something like:-

Smurf. Sorry you have to find out like this, but due to things out of our control we have had to close the firm down a bit rapid mate. Schenker will call us when you get this letter. Go to the yard and park up take everything out of the truck and trailer. There will be a welcome committee waiting for you when you get there, don't say anything just give them whatever they want. Leave the yard in the hire car and go round the back of the Royal Oak, we will see you there. And it was signed by all three of them, Sains, Spiller, and Worth.

There they were, all standing in the middle of the yard as we drove in. Scania, Rent co, Police, and Customs. We ignored the lot of them, got all our gear out then took everything out of the trailer boxes and put the lot over by the two Hertz rental cars. Then put all the papers for the truck and trailer on the fuel tank along with the keys, and handed the bond papers to the customs officer, and asked the bloke from Scania if he knew the way to Aberdeen, as that's where the load was for. But to make sure that it was road worthy first, and the trailer. Little jock has been looking under the slabs by the office and has found both sets of keys for the hire cars. All our gear in and we wave as we drive out and up the road to the Royal Oak pub, and park round the back. Into the saloon bar and order two pints of bitter. The three of them are sitting at the back of the bar waiting for us. They explain that it was due to all the dumped trailers and the drivers doing a bunk with the running money that they had to shut up shop, but we were getting paid. They stood up and gave us a large brown envelope, shook our hands and walked out.

Smurf and a rather tall Dane.

Mind the camel.

T.I.R Documents.

Passport with valid relevant visas.

Driving licence & International licence.

Insurance and Green card valid for Turkey

M.O.T for truck and trailer

G.V 60 Trailer I.D with photos

Carnet de Passage x2 truck & trailer

Carnet T.I.R International customs document

Cargo Manifest in English, German, and Arabic

Cargo invoices

C.M.R International delivery note

T.2 Customs document for fuel in belly tank

Permits for all countries to be crossed

All weights, quantities and values to match on each document. Manifest, CMR, Carnet TIR, and Invoices.

Total value of load must not exceed value of Carnet TIR.

Drivers Gear.

Good tool kit, 2x 5 ton jacks and timber blocks.

Tyre levers, wheel brace, tow bar, or tow chain

Spare wheels x2, filters (fuel & oil) light bulbs and lens

Fan and Alternator belts, Injector pipes, air lines

Electric lines, oil.

Gas cooker, pots and pans, kettle, mug and plate

Tined and fresh food in cool box

Bedding and blankets

Washing gear and towels

 Clothes for at least 4 weeks

Plenty of money.

www.ingramcontent.com/pod-product-compliance
Lightning Source LLC
Chambersburg PA
CBHW021154160426
42812CB00082B/3022/J